THE PRICE OF NEGLECT

Other titles by A.W. Tozer available from OM Publishing:

The Coming King
The Divine Conquest
God Tells the Man Who Cares
I Talk Back to the Devil
The Knowledge of the Holy
The Pursuit of God
The Root of the Righteous
Whatever Happened to Worship?
Who Put Jesus on the Cross?

THE PRICE OF NEGLECT

A.W. TOZER

publishing
CARLISLE, UK

This edition first published 1995
by arrangement with Christian Publications,
3825 Hartzdale Drive, Camp Hill, PA 17011, U.S.A.

01 00 99 98 97 96 95   7 6 5 4 3 2 1

OM Publishing is an imprint of Send the Light Ltd.,
P.O. Box 300, Carlisle, Cumbria CA3 0QS, U.K.

British Library Cataloguing in Publication Data

Tozer, A.W.
Price of Neglect
I. Title
248.5

ISBN 1-85078-200-8

Printed in the U.K. by Cox and Wyman Ltd., Reading

CONTENTS

FOREWORD

Anointed for This Generation

We know both from the Scriptures and from the history of the church that times of spiritual and moral declension are sure to come. It may be, as with us today, in the form of secularism, a muting or outright compromise of biblical truths, carnal worship or life styles practically identical with that of the world.

In such critical times God in His providence chose and "anointed" some person with a divine intuition, a built-in enablement to detect and decisively refuse whatever is basically incompatible with true biblical doctrine, spiritual worship and morality no matter who presents it or how it is set forth.

Such a divinely gifted person with consummate clarity, pointedness and skill calls God's true children to not follow the trends but to return to those teachings that are dear to the heart of God and to a transformation in the morals of persons and congregations.

Dr. A.W. Tozer, without question, had such an "anointing" for this generation. As an articulate preacher and perspicuous writer he assumed the role of a reverent forecaster. His so accurate description of unseemly religious and moral conditions and where they were leading the church are black facts that make one wonder about the "religion" in the evangelical church of our day.

His prophetic soul was impatient and even intractable in the face of the evangelical community's growing moral stupidity coupled with religious emotionalism and easy egoism. He decried that ". . . the whole evangelical world is to a large extent unfavorable to healthy Christianity. And I am not thinking of modernism either. I mean rather the Bible-believing crowd that bears the name of orthodoxy."

Nor was he quiescent when there arose those who claimed to have access to deeper teachings, to more esoteric truth, to a more reasonable theology, or to a more-compatible-with-the-times form of worship. More than any other, he dealt faithfully with sin and religious sham, rebuking anything that didn't square with Scripture. Also, with the illuminating flash of a mind literally steeped in the Word of God and exercised by the Holy Spirit, he was equally able to reveal the beauties of many a hidden truth and to so magnify the person and work of Christ that his auditors were awestruck.

Perhaps nothing finer could be said of Dr. Tozer than that he belonged to the great race of prophets and apostles. By nearly unanimous voice evangelical commentators have conferred on him the title, "The 20th Century Prophet."

Though he passed away in 1963, through this man's voluminous writings God continues to lay His hand on our minds and hearts. He possessed an aspiration and an inspiration and a spiritual aura which still influences a vast and admiring readership. While he lived, those of us who were privileged to know him well felt that here was a man who came forth from the inner place with its fragrance about him, though he himself seemed quite unconscious of it. This fragrance by divine alchemy is transmitted to us in his writings, of which this book is but a sample.

Probably no person now living is as well qualified to prepare a book of this nature as Harry Verploegh. Because of his long and close association with Dr. Tozer as friend, confidant and faithful partner, he has been able to sense what was in his mind and therefore make a splendid representative selection of his writings—excerpts compiled from his thought-provoking editorials and heart-searching sermons. Here then are vignettes of Dr. Tozer's thought which exerted such a wide-ranging influence and made such a profound impression on all sorts and conditions of people. His transparent sincerity, the literary charm of his style, his peculiar ability to communicate, his persuasive power in presenting Christ in the glory of His person, and in the fullness and fruitfulness of His work are all here for the reader to enjoy.

Louis L. King
President, (1978–1987)
The Christian and Missionary Alliance

CHAPTER
1

The Price of Neglect

Plato has somewhere said that in a democratic society the price wise men pay for neglecting politics is to be ruled by unwise men.

This observation is so patently true that no one who values his reputation for clear thinking is likely to contest it.

In America, for instance, there are millions of plain men and women, decent, honest and peace loving, who take their blessings for granted and make no effort to assure the continuance of our free society. These persons are without doubt far in the majority. They constitute the main body of our population, but for all their numbers they are not going to determine the direction our country will go in the next few years. Their weakness lies in their passivity. They sit back and allow radicals and those in the minority but who shout the loudest to set the course for the future. If this continues much longer we have no assurance that we can retain that liberty which was once purchased for us at such appalling cost.

The price good and sober Christians pay for doing nothing is to be led by those highly vocal minorities whose only qualifications for leadership are an overweening ambition and a loud voice. And there have always been and always will be such persons in the congregations of the saints. They know least and talk most, while sane and godly men too often give up leadership to them rather than to resist them. Later these same docile souls may shake their heads and lament their captivity. But by that time it is too late.

Within the circles of evangelical Christianity itself there has arisen in the last few years dangerous and dismaying trends away from true Bible Christianity. A spirit has been introduced which is surely not the Spirit of Christ, methods employed which are wholly carnal, objectives adopted which have not one line of Scripture to support them, a level of conduct accepted which is practically identical with that of the world—and yet scarcely one voice has been raised in opposition. And this in spite of the fact that the Bible-honoring followers of Christ lament among themselves the dangerous, wobbly course things are taking.

So radically is the essential spirit and content of orthodox Christianity changing these days under the vigorous leadership of undiscerning religionists that, if the trend is not stopped, what is called Christianity will soon be something altogether other than the faith of our fathers. We'll have only Bible words left. Bible religion will have perished from wounds received in the house of her friends.

The times call for a Spirit-baptized and articulate orthodoxy. They whose souls have been illuminated by the Holy Ghost must arise and under God assume leadership. There are those among us whose hearts can discern between the true and the false, whose spiritual sense of smell enables them to detect the spurious afar off, who have the blessed gift of *knowing*. Let such as these arise and be heard. Who knows but the Lord may return and leave a blessing behind Him?

CHAPTER
2

The Christian Funeral Needs a Reformation

We have long been of the opinion that for the blood-washed Christian the worst thing about dying is the funeral. Even among gospel Christians the funeral obsequies have degenerated into a gloomy ordeal that leaves everybody miserable for days. The only one not affected by the general heaviness that hangs over everything is the servant of God who has died and in whose honor the service is held. He has gone where the wicked cease from troubling and the weary be at rest. The minister and the undertaker, however, see to it that those who remain are neither untroubled nor at rest.

An odd contradiction exists here, for dolefulness is just what everybody is trying to avoid. Every effort is made to create the impression that the deceased is not really dead, and that the cemetery is not a graveyard at all but a pleasant park where everything is bright and full of cheer. Strangely enough, in spite of this obvious effort, the average funeral (even the Christian funeral) succeeds only in accenting the presence of death all the more. The dimmed lights, the low music, the smell of cut flowers, the unnatural tones of the minister and his slow march ahead of the coffin all contribute to the feeling of utter futility with which the service is charged.

We can't beat death by setting it to music. The instinct of the human heart is too strong to be cheated by little well-meant attempts to turn away its thoughts from the serious business of death and dying. Death is a solemn fact. Only unbelief or the insensibility caused by sin prevent the funeral of an unsaved man from being an agony of terror for his unsaved relatives. The honest minister can bring to the funeral of a lost man no real words of hope for the deceased. For the living there is hope, and the minster may do well to point them to the Savior, but if he has a proper regard for the sacredness of his office he will not give the living false hope concerning the dead.

The basic spirituality of any group of professed Christians may be discovered by observing the conduct of its advocates when faced with the harsh necessity of death. Where there is abounding gospel assurance among believers the funeral invariably takes on the air of a celebration rather than of a lamentation. Where that assurance is lacking, the whole atmosphere reveals it, however bravely the minister may quote, "There is no death, what seems so is transition." Where various ecclesiastical wires are pulled in an effort to secure last minute favors for the departed, where every attempt is made to placate death by timid posturing and ingratiating genuflections, we may be sure that the true gospel light has not shined. For a ransomed man knows how to die without crawling, and ransomed men know how to keep their poise in the presence of death.

The early Methodists enjoyed a degree of spiritual victory that lifted them above sorrow at the passing of their brethren. One of their funeral songs, for instance, ran like this:

Hosanna to Jesus on high!
  Another has entered her rest:
Another has 'scaped to the sky,
  And lodged in Immanuel's breast;
The soul of our sister is gone
  To heighten the triumph above;
Exalted to Jesus' throne,
  And clasped in the arms of his love.

Another song often heard when the Methodists lay away their beloved dead was this:

Weep not for a brother deceased;
  Our loss is his infinite gain;
A soul out of prison released,

And freed from its bodily chain;
With songs let us follow his flight,
And mount with his spirit above.
Escaped to the mansions of light,
And lodged in the Eden above.

How inferior the songs we sing today at the graves of our Christian dead. The note of joyous triumph is gone. The whole mood reflects the plaintive hopelessness of paganism. By our conduct at the funeral of those who sleep in Jesus we cancel out the testimony they gave while they lived. It is time for a change.

We share with other believers the hope that for many of us the return of Christ may circumvent death and project us into the Immaculate Presence without the necessity of dying. But if not, then let there be no gloomy faces among the few that gather to pay their last regards. We lived with the Resurrection in our heart and died in the Everlasting Arms. Hosanna! There's no room there for lamentation.

"I have observed," said the old historian, "that these Christians die well." A Christian can die well because he is the only one who dares to die at all. The lost man cannot afford to die, and that he must die is his infinite woe. A Christian dares to die because his Savior has died and risen. Let us renounce paganism at our funerals and die as we lived, like Christians.

CHAPTER

3

We Must Have True Faith

To many Christians Christ is little more than an idea, or at best an ideal; He is not a fact. Millions of professed believers talk as if He were real and act as if He were not. And always our actual position is to be discovered by the way we act, not by the way we talk.

We can prove our faith by our committal to it, and in no other way. Any belief that does not command the one who has it is not a real belief; it is a pseudo-belief only. And it might shock some of us profoundly if we were brought suddenly face to face with our beliefs and forced to test them in the fires of practical living.

Many of us Christians have become extremely skillful in arranging our lives so as to admit the truth of Christianity without being embarrassed by its implications. We fix things so that we can get on well enough without divine aid, while at the same time ostensibly seeking it. We boast in the Lord but watch carefully that we never get caught depending on Him. "The heart is deceitful above all things/ and beyond cure./ Who can understand it" (Jeremiah 17:9)?

Pseudo-faith always arranges a way out to serve in case God fails it. Real faith knows only one way and gladly allows itself to be stripped of any second ways or makeshift substitutes. For true faith, it is either God or total collapse. And not since Adam first stood up on the earth has God failed a single man or woman who trusted Him.

The man of pseudo-faith will fight for his verbal creed but refuse flatly to allow himself to get into a predicament where his future must depend upon that creed being true. He always provides himself with secondary ways of escape so he will have a way out if the roof caves in.

What we need very badly these days is a company of Christians who are prepared to trust God as completely now as they know they must do at the last day. For each of us the time is surely coming when we shall have nothing but God. Health and wealth and friends and hiding places will all be swept away and we shall have only God. To the man of pseudo-faith that is a terrifying thought, but to real faith it is one of the most comforting thoughts the heart can entertain.

It would be a tragedy indeed to come to the place where we have no other but God and find that we had not been trusting God at all during the days of our earthly sojourn. It would be better to *invite* God now to remove every false trust, to disengage our hearts from all secret hiding places and to bring us out into the open where we can discover for ourselves whether or not we really trust Him. That is a harsh cure for our troubles, but it is a sure one. Gentler cures may be too weak to do the work. And time is running out on us.

CHAPTER

4

Lyric Theology

Religious productions which come into being during times of great spiritual blessing are to be valued above those which appear during times of spiritual decline. Especially is this true if the production is a fair reflection of the spiritual state which prevails at the time it is written.

Examples are not hard to find. Take for instance the hymnody that sprang up around the Methodist revival of the 19th century. One hymnal put out by the Methodists lies at hand as we write. It was published in the year 1849. It contains 1,148 hymns, 553 of them written by Charles Wesley, and the amazing thing about the book is that there is hardly an inferior hymn in it. One quality which marks the hymns is the large measure of sound doctrine that is found in them. Quite a complete course in theology could be gotten from the hymnal alone without recourse to any other textbook.

The Holy Spirit was upon the Methodists in fullness of grace, and they sang of God and Christ and the Scriptures and of the mysteries and joys of redemption personally experienced. The hymnal is lyric theology, a theology that had been strained through the pores of the men and women who wrote and sang their joyous songs. The hymns are warm with the breath of worshipers, a breath that may still be detected fragrant upon them after the passing of a century.

Lay this hymnal beside almost any of the productions of the last 50 years and compare them. The differences will be found to be pronounced, and to the devout soul more than a little depressing. The last half-century has been for the most part a period of religious decline, and the hymnody which it has produced has expressed its low spiritual state. With the coming of the great religious campaigns, with their popular evangelists and their mass appeal, religious singing started on a long trip down, a trip which from all appearances has not yet ended. Experience took the place of theology in popular singing. Writers became more concerned with joy bells than with the blood of sprinkling. Ballad tunes displaced the graver and more serious type of melody. The whole spiritual mood declined and the songs expressed the mood faithfully.

At the risk of being written off as hopelessly outmoded, we venture to give it as our studied opinion that about the only good thing in the average modern songbook is the section of great hymns which most of them carry in the back—hymns which for the most part were written when the Church was at her flood and which are included now as a gesture of respect to the past, and rarely sung.

CHAPTER
5

Hobab's Eyes

During the early days of the wilderness journey of the Israelites an odd and significant transaction took place between Moses and an in-law named Hobab.

> Now Moses said to Hobab . . . "We are setting out for the place about which the Lord said, 'I will give it to you.' Come with us and we will treat you well." . . . He answered, "No, I will not go; I am going back to my own land and my own people." But Moses said, "Please do not leave us. You know where we should camp in the desert, and you can be our eyes. If you come with us, we will share with you whatever good things the Lord gives us." (Numbers 10:29–32)

Imagine! Moses hired a guide to lead Israel through the wilderness! The circumstances being what they were, this seems almost incredible, but Moses was a man capable of making mistakes like the rest of us. And hiring Hobab was a serious mistake. Here is why.

God had already told Moses that He himself would lead Israel into the promised land. "See, I am sending an Angel ahead of you to guard you along the way and to bring you to the place I have prepared" (Exodus 23:20). God had also provided the wondrous cloud and fire to lead them (Numbers 9:15–23). Furthermore, in the very chapter that tells of Moses' effort to enlist Hobab's aid it is written, "So they set out from the mountain of the Lord and traveled for three days. The ark of the covenant of the Lord went before them those three days to find them a place to rest" (Numbers 10:33). So through the divinely appointed angel and by means of the ark and the cloudy pillar *God Himself was guiding Israel through the wilderness.* What need then had they of Hobab's eyes?

Hobab was not to blame for his part in this strange doing, but his presence added nothing to the safety of the marching army; and there is reason to believe that he may have been a spiritual stumbling block both to Moses and to the nation of Israel. The more they trusted to Hobab the less they trusted in God. And that was bad for Israel.

The Church also has her appointed Guide to lead her in her earthly journey. "But the Counselor, the Holy Spirit, whom the Father will send in my name, will teach you all things and will remind you of everything I have said to you" (John 14:26). "Because those who are led by the Spirit of God are sons of God" (Romans 8:14). These and a wealth of other Scriptures assure us that we are under the direct care of the Holy Spirit. Safety and fruitfulness require only that we accept the leadership of God. Blessing lies in the way of submission and obedience.

What need do we have of Hobab's eyes? Surely none at all. Yet the Church has a whole army of Hobabs to which it looks eagerly for guidance and leadership. That Hobab has no place in the divine plan never seems to matter at all. That Hobab is an intruder, that his eyes are not sharp enough to search out the path, that he is altogether superfluous and actually in the way is passed over by almost everyone. God seems so far away, the Bible is such an old book, faith makes such heavy demands upon our flesh, and Hobab is so near at hand and so real and easy to lean on—so we act like men of earth instead of like men of heaven, and Hobab gets the job.

Now, who is Hobab? and how can we identify him? The answer is easy. Hobab is anything gratuitously introduced into the holy work of God which does not have biblical authority for its existence. At first this new thing may seem innocent enough and even look like an improvement over the biblical pattern; and because it is new it is sure to catch on fast and spread quickly among the churches.

We Christians are soon playing "follow the leader," trotting along docilely behind Hobab and justifying his presence by appealing to his popularity. Anyone as popular as Hobab cannot be wrong, no matter how far he may be from the Word of God.

Hobab is not an individual. He is whatever takes our attention from the cloud and fire; he is whatever causes us to lean less heavily upon God and look less trustfully to the guiding Spirit. Each one of us must look out for him in our own life and in our church. And when we discover him we must get rid of him right away.

CHAPTER
6

On Brother Lawrence

One of the purest souls ever to live on this fallen planet was Nicholas Herman, that simplehearted Christian, known throughout the world as Brother Lawrence.

He wrote very little, but what he wrote has seemed to several generations of Christians to be so rare and so beautiful as to deserve a place near the top among the world's great books of devotion. So well is he established in the affection of spiritual souls of all denominations and every shade of Christian thought that it is hardly too much to say that the expressions of an adverse opinion of Brother Lawrence may be taken as evidence that the critic is either a victim of his own prejudices, or is too engrossed with this world even to understand the spirit of a man as heavenly-minded as he.

Early in his life Brother Lawrence found Christ as his own Savior and Lord and entered into what he called "the unspeakable riches of God and of Jesus Christ." He was a common cook but he learned to turn the modest service into a kind of worship. "We can do little things for God," he said. "I turn the cake that is frying on the pan for love of Him, and that done, if there is nothing else to call me, I prostrate myself in worship before Him who has given me grace to work. Afterwards I rise happier than a king."

He spent his long life walking in the presence of His Lord, and when he came to die there was no need for any particular change in his occupation. At the last hour someone asked him what was going on in his thoughts as death approached. He replied simply: "I am doing what I shall do through all eternity—blessing God, praising God, adoring God, giving Him the love of my whole heart. It is our one business, my brethren, to worship Him and love Him without thought of anything else."

The writings of Brother Lawrence are the ultimate in simplicity. His teachings knew very little variety, and consisted mostly of a few great ideas woven like costly threads to make a pattern of great beauty.

CHAPTER

7

Our Low Level of Moral Enthusiasm Part I

Were some watcher or holy one from the bright world above to come among us for a time with the power to diagnose the spiritual ills of church people there is one entry which I am quite sure would appear on the vast majority of his reports: *Definite evidence of chronic spiritual lassitude; level of moral enthusiasm extremely low.*

What makes this condition especially significant is that Americans are not naturally an unenthusiastic people. Indeed they have a worldwide reputation for being just the opposite. Visitors to our shores from other countries never cease to marvel at the vigor and energy with which we attack our problems. We live at a fever pitch, and whether we are erecting buildings, laying highways, promoting athletic events, celebrating special days or welcoming returning heroes we always do it with an exaggerated flourish. Our building will be taller, our highway broader, our athletic contest more colorful, our celebration more elaborate and more expensive than would be true anywhere else on earth. We walk faster, drive faster, earn more, spend more and run a higher blood pressure than almost any other people in the world.

In only one field of human interest are we slow and apathetic; that is the field of personal religion. There for some strange reason our enthusiasm flags. Church people habitually approach the matter of their personal relation to God in a dull, halfhearted way which is altogether out of keeping with their general temperament and wholly inconsistent with the importance of the subject.

It is true that there is a lot of religious activity among us. Interchurch basketball tournaments, religious splash parties followed by devotions, weekend camping trips with a Bible quiz around the fire, Sunday school picnics, building fund drives and ministerial breakfasts are with us in unbelievable numbers, and they are carried on with typical American gusto. It is when we enter the sacred precincts of the heart's personal religion that we suddenly lose all enthusiasm.

So we find this strange and contradictory situation: a world of noisy, headlong religious activity carried on without moral energy or spiritual fervor. In a year's travel among the churches one scarcely finds a believer whose blood count is normal and whose temperature is up to standard. The flush and excitement of the soul in love must be sought in the New Testament or in the biographies of the saints; we look for them in vain among the professed followers of Christ in our day.

Now if there is any reality within the whole sphere of human experience that is by its very nature worthy to challenge the mind, engross and charm the heart and bring the total life to a burning focus it is the reality that revolves and shines around the person of Christ. If He is who and what the Christian message declares Him to be, then the thought of Him should be the most exciting, the most stimulating, to enter the human mind. It is not hard to understand how Paul could join wine and the Spirit in one verse, "Do not get drunk on wine, which leads to debauchery. Instead, be filled with the Spirit" (Ephesians 5:18). When the Spirit presents Christ to our inner vision it has an exhilarating effect on the soul much as wine has on the body. The Spirit-filled man may literally dwell in a state of spiritual vivacity amounting to a mild and pure inebriation.

God dwells in a state of perpetual enthusiasm. He is delighted with all that is good and lovingly concerned about all that is wrong. He pursues His labors always in a fullness of holy zeal. No wonder the Spirit came at Pentecost as the sound of a rushing, mighty wind and sat in tongues of fire on every forehead. In so doing He was acting in character with His position as one of the Persons of the blessed Godhead.

Whatever else happened at Pentecost, one thing that cannot be missed by the most casual observer was the sudden upsurging of moral enthusiasm. Those first disciples burned with a steady inward fire. They were enthusiastic to the point of complete abandon.

Dante, on his imaginary journey through hell, came upon a group of lost souls who sighed and moaned continually as they whirled about aimlessly in the dusky air. Virgil, his guide, explained that these were the "wretched people," the "nearly soulless," who while they lived on earth had not moral energy enough to be either good or evil. They had earned neither praise nor blame. And with them and sharing in their punishment were those angels who would take sides neither with God nor Satan. The doom of all of the weak and irresolute crew was to be suspended forever between a hell that despised them and a heaven that would not receive their defiled presence. Not even their names were to be mentioned again in heaven or earth or hell. "Look," said the guide, "and pass on."

Was Dante saying in his own way what our Lord had said long before to the church of Laodicea, "I know your deeds, that you are neither cold nor hot: I wish you were either one or the other! So, because you are lukewarm—

neither hot nor cold—I am about to spit you out of my mouth" (Revelation 3:15–16)?

The low level of moral enthusiasm among us may have a significance far deeper than we are willing to believe.

CHAPTER
8

Our Low Level of Moral Enthusiasm Part II

One marked characteristic of present-day Christians is the low level of their spiritual energy, their all but total lack of moral enthusiasm.

I do not believe that it is necessary to prove this. We carry the proof in our own hearts and observe it in the conduct of our Christian friends. We may safely accept it as a fact and go on from there.

Back of this condition I believe there are four principal causes. They are:

1. A deadened sense of sin in the Church. The very word *sin* is not in good standing in present-day philosophy and psychology. The intellectuals have put us on the defensive and have made us ashamed to believe in sin as a reality. It is somewhat like believing in nymphs or kelpies, quite all right for a less educated generation but surely not in keeping with our advanced scientific knowledge. The relativity

of morals has been taught to our college youth for a long enough period to give the idea time to sift down into the mind of the man on the street and affect the whole popular concept of right and wrong. Hence there is no sharp line drawn between good and evil, even among church people.

2. The result is that when people "accept" Christ they do so with little or no real conviction for sin and without radical repentance. It is rare now to see a transforming conversion. The average convert becomes one by a series of compromises, whereby he surrenders something to gain something and dickers for his salvation like a huckster. The thought of unconditional surrender to the Lordship of Jesus never enters his mind. A shoddy mercantile theology has reduced the whole thing to the level of an across-the-counter transaction with no loss of face to the sinner. Of course the resultant conversion is a cold-blooded, emotionless affair.

3. Next in order and flowing directly out of these is the absence of an experiential encounter with the living God. The personal encounter gave fire and life to the religion of the Bible. "Abram fell on his face: and God talked with him." Jacob met God on two occasions and those meetings affected him as light affects a sensitized plate. Moses trembled before God in delighted fear. The Bible itself grew out of such experiences. They were not alike except in

their spiritual content and their clear and lasting effect upon the individual heart. This content is so weak among Christians today as to be all but unrecognizable. The significant words of prophet and apostle were "I saw . . . I heard . . . the heavens were opened . . . I saw the Lord," and other like expressions. Today we try to substitute a pale, waxy "faith" for such vivid encounters. No wonder the Church has taken on the general tone of a convalescent hospital instead of the camp of a victorious army.

4. The fourth cause of our lack of moral enthusiasm, as I see it, is the absence from our experience of an object for the heart's devotion. The great spiritual souls of other days had such an object. In the Old Testament they were frankly and unashamedly in love with the Most High God, and when He became flesh and dwelt among us He came still nearer to the hearts of His people. Paul's heart exploded into a burning volcano of love for the Lord Jesus. It was this and not his theology alone that made him the fiery spirit he was. This it was that gave us Augustine, Bernard, Francis, Rolle, Rutherford and the rest of the shining company.

Today we find ourselves on the fourth step of the chilly stairs that lead downward: 1. No conviction for sin. 2. No transforming conversion. 3. No encounter with God. 4. No object of worship. Where do we go from here?

CHAPTER

9

God Loves Us in His Son

For those who think beneath the surface of things there are some real problems associated with the doctrine of the love of God. What is by many so airily taken for granted because it has been so often repeated is found to hold some positive difficulties when it is examined by the thoughtful and serious-minded Christian.

The first difficulty is one that is likely to bother the soul that is deeply convinced of its own grave sinfulness and its complete unworthiness before God. The problem simply stated is, "How can God love anyone as sinful and worthless as I am?" This question occurs in many of our hymns and is heard in countless prayers and testimonies wherever a group of humble believers come together.

It is not likely that the question will ever be answered to the satisfaction of the penitent heart, for whatever theology says it will always feel its own deep sinfulness and will side against itself and acknowledge that God would be just were He to forsake it forever. Because this is an impulse of the heart and springs not out of reason but out of moral repugnance, there is not much that reason can do to correct it. And I wonder if, after all, we want to eliminate this emotion from the heart entirely. Self-loathing may be carried too far, but a little of it keeps us down where we belong. I think the great saints have always felt it to some degree.

The second problem is a more serious one. It is this: How can a holy God love unholy men? This should not be dismissed lightly, for it involves a real theological predicament. God loves and must love what is like Himself. Now since He is by nature perfectly holy how can He love that which is by nature completely unholy? Man being deceitful above all things and desperately wicked, with every imagination of the thoughts of his heart only evil continually, how can that God who is exactly the opposite of all this find in the sinner anything to love? Would not God's love for that which is radically unlike Himself constitute a moral contradiction and put Him in the position of compromising His holiness?

Of course this is no problem to the quasi-religious person who thinks of God as a great "All-Father" or as merely a kindly spirit that pervades the world, without holiness, justice or truth. A weak, sniveling god who is too loving to condemn sin would have no trouble loving sinners. He could not compromise his holiness for the simple reason that he does not possess any. Such a god is the darling of the starry-eyed religious poet whose "creed is love," but he is most surely not the God of the Bible. He is a figment of a fallen and darkened imagination and is as certainly false as were the gods of the Philistines.

To the question, "How can a holy God love an unholy sinner?" there is a full and satisfactory answer. The answer, of course, is found in the teachings of the Scripture. It has been stated for us by the German theologian Eckhart: "The Father loves nothing at all but the Son and such things as He finds in the Son." This is a fair summation of the doctrine of the love of God as presented on the pages of Holy Writ.

"The Father loves nothing at all but the Son." All the love of God is gathered up in Christ. The Father loves the Son with all the love there is, which is to say with all of Himself, and He loves *directly* nothing but the Son. In the Son and through the Son all things came into being, including man. God loves men not for themselves but for the sake of the Son. His love for them is reflected from the face of Jesus Christ and falls upon them only as they are related to the Son. Man was made in God's image and Christ is said to be "the image of the invisible God."

In some mysterious way is the race of

mankind related to the Son, and for His sake God can lavish His love upon sinful men and still be just and holy in doing so.

A marginal problem, of no practical importance, is whether or not God continues to love sinners after they have forfeited their rights under the patient forbearance of God and have been consigned to their final place in hell. To believe that He does would be to conceive of Him as being eternally frustrated. Were He to continue forever to pour upon lost men an unrequited love, He could never be at rest. His wasted love would torture Him without end forever.

The truth is that God loves only the Son "and such things as He finds in the Son." When impenitent men have made their final decision against the Son and have walked out of His light for good they will no longer be objects of the love of God. God's love is, like Himself, unchanging and eternal, but it touches only those who touch the Son. The soul that rejects the Son by a final irrevocable act forfeits forever the love of the Father.

CHAPTER

10

Personal Holiness Is First

A selfish desire for happiness is as sinful as any other selfish desire. Its root is in the flesh which can never have any standing before God. "The sinful mind is hostile to God. It does not submit to God's law nor can it do so" (Romans 8:7).

People are coming more and more to excuse every sort of wrongdoing on the grounds that they are "just trying to secure a little happiness." Before she will give her consent to marriage the modern young lady may ask outright whether or not the man "can make me happy." The lovelorn columns of the newspapers are wet with the self-pitying tears of persons who write to inquire how they can "preserve their happiness." The psychiatrists of the land are getting fat off the increasing numbers who seek professional aid in their all-absorbing search for happiness. It is not uncommon for crimes to be committed against persons who do nothing worse than "jeopardize" someone's happiness.

This is the hedonistic philosophy of old Grecian days misunderstood and applied to everyday living in the 20th century. It destroys all nobility of character and makes milksops of all who consciously or unconsciously adopt it; but is quite the popular creed of the masses. That we are born to be happy is scarcely questioned by anyone. No one bothers to prove that fallen men have any moral right to happiness, or that they are in the long run any better off happy. The only question before the house is how to get the most happiness out of life. The thesis of almost all popular books and plays is that personal happiness is the legitimate end of the dramatic human struggle.

Now, I submit that the whole hectic scramble after happiness is an evil as certainly as is the scramble after money or fame or success. It springs out of a vast misunderstanding of ourselves and of our true moral condition. No one who really knows himself can ever believe in his right to be happy. A little glimpse of his own heart will disillusion him instantly so that he is more likely to turn on himself and own God's sentence against him to be just. The doctrine of man's inalienable right to happiness is anti-God and anti-Christ, and its wide acceptance by society tells us a lot about that same society.

The effect of this modern hedonism is felt also among the people of God. The gospel is too often presented as a means toward happiness, to peace of mind or security. There are even those who use the Bible to "relax" them, as if it were a drug.

How far wrong all this is will be discovered easily by the simple act of reading the New Testament through once with meditation. There the emphasis is not upon happiness but upon holiness. God is more concerned with the state of people's hearts than with the state of their feelings. Undoubtedly the will of God brings much final happiness to those who obey, but the most important matter is not how happy we are but how holy. The soldier does not seek to be happy; he seeks rather to get the fighting over with, to win the war and get back home to his loved ones. There he may enjoy himself to the full; but while the war is on his most pressing job is to be a good soldier, to acquit himself like a man, regardless of how he feels.

The childish clamor after happiness can become a real snare. One may easily deceive himself by cultivating a religious joy without a correspondingly righteous life. No man should desire to be happy who is not at the same time holy. He should spend his efforts in seeking to know and do the will of God, leaving to Christ the matter of how happy he shall be.

For those who take this whole thing seriously I have a suggestion. Go to God and have an understanding. Tell Him that it is your desire to be holy at any cost and then ask Him never to give you more happiness than holiness. When your holiness becomes tarnished, let you joy become dim. And ask Him to make you holy whether you are happy or not. Be assured that in the end you will be as happy as you are holy; but for the time being let your whole ambition be to serve God and be Christlike. If we are to take a stand like that we may expect to know a new degree of inward purification and, God being who He is, we are more than likely to know a new degree of happiness as well, but a happiness that springs out of a more intimate fellowship with God, a happiness that is elevated and unselfish and free from the carnal drawings of the flesh.

CHAPTER

11

Let's Not Take It for Granted

A little Sunday school song popular a few years ago exhorted us in moments of discouragement to count our many blessings, and it assured us that if we did so we would be astonished at the many things the Lord had done for us.

The song itself is hardly a classic, but it does contain more than a little practical wisdom. We are by nature inclined to be ungrateful and to take as a matter of course the countless blessings God every day showers upon us. We need to keep our thankfulness alive by reminding ourselves how many benefits we enjoy, both as individuals and as a nation.

First, we should be thankful for the Church. With all its faults, the Church has kept the torch of truth burning so that today no one in the civilized world need be in darkness. No one who reads these words but can have abundance of spiritual light if he is interested enough to seek it. Even in these days of declension there are still enough gospel churches to illuminate the public mind. Spiritual darkness where it occurs is the result of indifference. There is plenty of light. The Spirit in the Church has seen to that. And for this we should be deeply grateful.

Then we should be thankful for our country. There is real danger that the doings of cheap politicians should sour us against our own land. Charges and countercharges are being hurled back and forth till the air is blue with them. We must guard against becoming cynical and losing faith in America. Without approving everything we see, there is still sound reason to thank God for our country and all it stands for.

Among the treasures enjoyed by all of us is freedom. Though greatly maligned by its foes and deeply wounded in the house of its friends, it is yet the sweetest thing under the sun next to the Christian religion. Only those who have lost it can fully appreciate it. We are so used to being free that we are in danger of taking our freedom for granted. Let us never do so. We are free at the cost of blood. Many thousands of brave men, who loved life as dearly as we, lie sleeping row on row on a hundred battlefields. They secured for us the right to walk in the sun and to breathe the sweet air of heaven. We should never think of them without bowing our heads in respect to them and in gratitude to God.

For our family also we should each one be thankful. Usually we live too close to our own people to appreciate them as we should. Only after they have left us do we discover how much we owe them. The home is our nursery, our first school, our refuge from life's rough winds and our resting place after the toils of the day. Allowing for its inevitable imperfections, the family and the home are dear beyond words. Father, mother, sister, brother—how much we owe them and how little we repay. Thanksgiving should remind us that our own people mean more than we, in our busy preoccupation, are likely to remember.

To our friends and neighbors also we owe a big debt of gratitude. The most "friendless" man, if he will but stop a moment, is likely to discover how many friends he really has after all. Only the man who has like a rogue elephant turned against the herd and put himself outside the bounds of human tolerance may be said to be wholly friendless. And even he may be treated with the most unexpected kindness by policemen, judges and jailers. If the members of society are forced to turn their backs upon the outlaw they seldom do it with bitterness. For the most vicious criminal there remains yet a tattered remnant of love and sympathy.

If this is true of the morally abandoned how much more may the average decent citizen expect and receive understanding and affection.

The newspapers know from long experience that a picture of an orphaned baby will bring a hundred inquiries from sympathetic parents who want to adopt it. The story of a needy family will bring in a truckload of gifts from the readers.

And for us Christians, how much closer and dearer are our friendships. They begin here on earth and continue beyond death and enter the world above. For our Christian friends we should be tenderly thankful, and more so as the years go on. We should never take them for granted. They are much too precious for that.

Lastly, because most precious of all, is the friendship and communion of Jesus. He is the friend that sticketh closer than a brother and He has assured us that He will never leave us nor forsake us. Let this knowledge keep us ever thankful. We dare not take Jesus for granted. His love alone should keep the flame of our gratitude at white heat until that day when we shall be presented to the Father with exceeding joy.

CHAPTER

12

There Are Two Sides to the Christian Life

The old devotional writers used to say that there are two kinds of Christian life, the active and the contemplative. And their favorite illustration was the story of Mary and Martha.

Martha stood for the active life, and Mary for the contemplative. The first was concerned with practical service and the second with worship. Of course the contemplative life as represented by Mary was preferred over the other. Martha came to stand for a shallow if useful type of Christian life and the emphasis was placed upon the superiority of the life of prayer and meditation as Mary lived it. Naturally she, not Martha, was held up for emulation.

Now the truth is that Christians cannot be divided into two types and no more, as if Martha does nothing but cook and Mary sits always at Jesus' feet. Human beings are not as simple as that. The most heavenly person must break off meditation sometimes to attend to pressing earthly needs, and the most active Christian must retire sometimes to recharge his spiritual batteries. We are not forced to accept the familiar either/or, to choose to be either a praying Christian or a working one, as if it were not possible to be both. Actually every true Christian *is* both to some degree. The problem is one of balance.

The anonymous author of the celebrated *Cloud of Unknowing*, though very emphatically on the side of the detached, worshiping life, nevertheless admits that the two aspects of the Christian life may be fused into one. "There be," he writes, "two manner of lives in Holy Church. The one is active life, the other is contemplative life. Active is the lower, and contemplative is the higher. Active life hath two degrees, a higher and a lower: and also contemplative life hath two degrees, a lower and a higher. Also these two lives be so coupled together that although they be diverse in some part, yet neither of them may be fully without some part of the other. For why? That part that is the higher part of active life, that same part is the lower part of contemplative life. So that a man may not be fully active, but if he be in part contemplative; nor yet fully contemplative . . . if he be not in part active."

Stated in modern terms this means simply that every real Christian, however practical, is in some degree a mystic, his mysticism lying on the upper side of his life. He prays, meditates on spiritual things and communes with God and the invisible world. Also, every Christian, however he may be dedicated to the holy art of prayer and worship, must of necessity descend to work and eat and sleep and pay his taxes and get on somehow with the hard world around him. And if he follows on to know the Lord he must serve in every useful way outlined for him in the Scriptures of truth. To be a Christian it is necessary that he serve his generation as well as his God.

The big problem is to keep the two elements of the Christian life in proper balance. Martha and Mary are sisters and we need both. During the years since Pentecost one and then another of the two has had her day to the exclusion of the other. The pendulum has swung from the practical to the mystical and back again with the passing of the years, and while both sides of the religious life were always present, one side or the other usually got all the attention at a given time. Too bad that even religion must be influenced by intellectual and spiritual fashions.

Today the Christian emphasis falls heavily on the "active" life. People are more concerned with earth than with heaven; they would rather "do something" than to commune with God. The average Christian feels a lot nearer to this world than to the world above. The current vogue favors "Christian action." The favorite brand of Christianity is that sparked by the man in a hurry, hard hitting, aggressive and ready with the neat quip. We are neglecting the top side of our souls. The light in the tower burns dimly while we hurry about the grounds below, making a great racket and giving the impression of wonderful devotion to our task.

The difficult part of this whole thing is to get people to see what is happening to us. The average Christian has accepted the prevailing spiritual mood as normal and is likely to become indignant with anyone who dares to question its soundness or to suggest that the Christian religion as we experience it today is not in every particular one and the same as the religion of the apostles.

It is time that we prayerfully test the flavor of present Christianity and compare its spiritual quality with that of the New Testament. I think we shall find the element of mystic worship all but absent from it. I say all but absent, for it can never be wholly absent. Wherever the Spirit of Christ is present, however imperfectly perceived, the sense of worship will be there in some slight degree.

It is to our lasting reproach that we cannot live full rounded and symmetrical lives, embodying in our redeemed personalities the practical service of Martha and the adoring vision of Mary. We would appear to be unwilling to have both sisters present at once. Just now Martha is all over the premises, but where is Mary? I wish someone would find her soon.

CHAPTER
13

Economic Considerations Kill Religion

Demetrius, the silversmith, could offer no other proof of the truth of his religion than to shout, "Sirs, ye know that by this craft we have our wealth. . . . Great is Diana of the Ephesians!" He encouraged Diana-worship for economic reasons.

An economic interest in religion is deadly. As soon as a man becomes thus entangled in the snare of economic interest he is a true prophet no longer, but a son of mammon. His heart degenerates and his spirit begins to die. Let him perform a religious duty, do a moral act, advocate a reform, or preach a doctrine because he must do so to guarantee his income, and he is no true shepherd now, but a hireling.

That the Church should support its ministers as a country supports its soldiers to free them for the battle is taken for granted by almost all Christians. This arrangement is found in the Old Testament and is carried over into the

Church with little change. It is a wise and sound procedure and is above reproach so long as both priest and people are true children of God.

A grave obligation lies upon the church to keep the minister financially free to teach what he from the heart believes. The economic boycott is a weapon sometimes used against the man who insists upon preaching unwelcome truth, and pity the man who is caught in it. Pity more, however, the church that would stoop to exercise it.

Paul had a trade upon which he could fall back when and if the need arose, and I am not sure but it would be a good idea for every preacher to keep a needle and thread handy in case of emergency. Anything is better than to do obeisance to mammon.

A few preachers have found a happy solution to the economic problem in the simple plan of living by faith. No one can put the economic squeeze on such a man; for as he is accountable to God alone for his ministry, God is, by the same token, responsible for his daily bread. It is impossible to starve a man into submission under this arrangement, for the servant of God lives on manna, and manna can be found wherever faith can see it.

CHAPTER

14

Prayer Changes People—and Things

No one who has read the Bible with any perception can fail to see that to God men are more important than things. A human being is of more value than a thousand galaxies of stars or a million worlds like ours. God made man in His own image and He made *things* to serve man. His concern is with intelligent moral beings, not with lifeless matter.

However, since man has a material body and must live out his days in an environment of matter, time and space, *things* are important to him. His earthly life is to a large degree interwoven with matter and the laws that control matter. He is often deeply affected by the report his senses bring him from the world around him. Situations sometimes develop where the welfare of the inner man is for the time allowed to depend somewhat upon outward circumstances. At such times it is altogether proper that he should pray to God to alter those circumstances and "change things" to afford a more favorable climate for the growth of the spirit. A thousand promises are recorded in the Scriptures to encourage him to ask and seek and knock to the end that unfavorable things might be changed or removed altogether. And the history of Israel and the Church abundantly demonstrates that God does hear and answer prayer.

In all our praying, however, it is important that we keep in mind that God will not alter His eternal purposes at the word of a man. We do not pray in order to persuade God to change His mind. Prayer is not an assault upon the reluctance of God, nor an effort to secure a suspension of His will for us or for those for whom we pray. Prayer is not intended to overcome God and "move His arm." God will never be other than Himself, no matter how many people pray, nor how long nor how earnestly.

God's love desires the best for all of us, and He desires to give us the best at any cost. He will open rivers in desert places, still turbulent waves, quiet the wind, bring water from the rock, send an angel to release an apostle from prison, feed an orphanage, open a land long closed to the gospel. All these things and a thousand others He has done and will do in answer to prayer, but only because it had been His will to do it from the beginning. No one persuades Him.

What the praying man does is to bring his

will into line with the will of God so God can do what He has all along been willing to do. Thus prayer changes the man and enables God to change things in answer to man's prayer.

CHAPTER

15

Three Factors That Make a Deed Good

Every Christian wants to do good. He knows that he is not saved by his good deeds, but he knows also that good deeds will follow his salvation and be the practical proof that it is real. And he knows that he will someday stand before the judgment seat of Christ to receive the consequences of deeds done in the body, whether they be good or evil.

To be good a deed must pass three tests: What? Why? and How? What we do is, of course, important. There are deeds that are wrong in themselves; nothing can make them right and no circumstances can excuse them. Such we will pass by for the moment and give our attention to those acts that are considered good without question by the generality of mankind.

At the risk of being thought repetitious I'll say again that in religion and morals motive comes very near to being everything. It is not *what* a man does only but *why* he does it that determines the moral quality of the deed. A deed which on the surface may be good, if done for a selfish reason is actually evil. And since we cannot often penetrate to the springs of human conduct we cannot always be sure whether the deeds of others are good or bad. Charity dictates that we give every man the advantage of the doubt, but God alone knows the facts. I trust that most of us serve God and our fellow men from motives that will stand the test of Why?

But there is another factor about which I find it impossible to be wholly optimistic. It is *how* our good deeds are done; that is, the spirit in which we do them. I think it is possible to pass the first two tests and fail the third dismally.

Above all persons the Christian should be gracious and self-effacing. His alms should be given in private and as unostentatiously as possible. He should avoid making the recipient feel embarrassed. A loan may be made, for instance, in such a manner that the one who receives it may be humiliated and hurt so deeply that the later repayment of the loan will not square the transaction. He will feel cheap and inferior for a long time simply because the loan was made in a wrong spirit.

A little poem says in few words what I have in mind:

Inglorious
  And a shame to see,

Is a favor done
  Ungraciously.

I am afraid there are a great many favors done so ungraciously as to be no favors at all but actual injuries to the persons receiving them. Most of us at some time have had the painful experience of being made to feel small by a favor done with a superior air or a tolerant smile. We Christians should study and pray for the grace of casualness when helping a friend. I have known a few persons who have been able to do a favor in such a way as to create the feeling that they themselves were being favored. Such an art is as rare as it is beautiful. We should cultivate it more carefully.

It is scarcely necessary to point out that a contribution made grudgingly will not be accepted by the Lord. A sour gift is no gift at all even if it is given to the poor or to foreign missions. Religious work done under protest might as well be left undone. It is not good in fact, however excellent it may seem to be.

The sum of the matter is that our works, to be good, must have our hearts in them. They must be the works of the Spirit, done in the Spirit. Short of this they are but wood, hay and stubble.

CHAPTER

16

No Christian Should Feel Contempt

One of the hardest sayings in the New Testament is this: "Anyone who says to his brother, 'Raca,' is answerable to the Sanhedrin [council, KJV]. But anyone who says, 'You fool!' will be in danger of the fire of hell" (Matthew 5:22b).

What our Lord is saying here is not that a man will be punished with hell fire for calling another a fool, but that a man who can say "You fool" to a fellow man is revealing a state of heart which will fit him for hell in the end. Not the relatively slight offense of calling a brother a fool, but the serious sin of *contempt* endangers a man's future. The gravity of the situation lies not in the fact that a man can cry "Fool!" but that he can feel the contempt which the word expresses.

Contempt for a human being is an affront to God almost as grave as idolatry, for while idolatry is disrespect for God Himself, contempt is disrespect for the being He made in

His own image. Contempt says of a man, "*Raca!* This fellow is of no worth. I attach to his person no value whatsoever." The man guilty of thus appraising a human being is thoroughly bad; and for a number of reasons.

Contempt is an emotion possible only where there is great pride. The error in moral judgment that undervalues another always springs out of the error that overvalues oneself. The contemptuous man esteems himself too highly for reasons that are invalid. His high opinion of himself is not based upon his position as a being made in God's image; he esteems himself for fancied virtues which he does not possess. He is wrong in his attitude toward himself and doubly wrong in his estimation of his fellow man. The error in his judgment is moral, not intellectual.

It is in the realm of religion that contempt finds its most fruitful soil and flourishes most luxuriantly. It is seen in the cold disdain with which the respectable church woman regards the worldly sister and in the scorn heaped upon the fallen woman by the legally married wife. The sober deacon may find it hard to conceal his contempt for the neighbor who drinks. The evangelical may castigate the liberal in a manner that leaves slight doubt that he feels himself above him in every way. Religion that is not purified by penitence, humility and love, will lead to a feeling of contempt for the irreligious and the morally degraded. And since contempt implies a judgment of no worth made against a human brother, the contemptuous man comes under the displeasure of God and proves himself to lie in danger of hell fire.

The Christian cannot close his eyes to good and evil in his fellow men. He cannot avoid rendering moral judgment on the deeds of men; and, indeed, he is accountable to do so. "By their fruits ye shall know them." "From such turn away." But his disapprobation of the evil ways of men must not betray him into contempt for their humanity. He must reverence the humanity of every man, however degraded, out of appreciation for his divine origin. No one for whom Christ died can be common or worthless. Humanity itself must be honored as the garment assumed by the Eternal Son in the Incarnation. To esteem anyone worthless who wears the form of a man is to be guilty of an affront to the Son of Man. We should hate sin in ourselves and in all men, but we should never undervalue the man in whom the sin is found.

CHAPTER

17

We Must Be Church-Minded

So precious is the Church in the eyes of God that it is scarcely possible it should ever become too precious in the eyes of men. "I love Thy Church, O God," should be next after "I love Thee, O Lord."

The Church is the temple in which the Spirit of Christ dwells, the body of which Christ is the Head, the medium through which He works for the reclamation of mankind. Individual members of the Church working in harmony with each other are the lips and hands and feet of the inliving Christ. The Church is the true Shekinah, the visible habitation of the invisible God, the Bride of Christ, destined to share forever the love of His heart and the privileges of His throne.

It is, of course, not possible at this time to have the whole together again "all with one accord in one place." Some of her members have gone to join the Church of the Firstborn in heaven and now mingle with the spirits of just men made perfect. And they who still remain on earth form a company too vast ever to assemble in one building. The gathering of the whole Church in one place must wait the consummation. Only the city four-square will provide sufficient room for such a joyous assembly.

While the whole Church cannot come together on earth, God has ordered it so that the same thing can be realized on a limited scale by the gathering together of small groups of believers in the fellowship of worship and prayer. Any assembly of true Christians is a church. "For where two or three come together in my name, there am I with of them" (Matthew 18:20). The name and the Presence are indispensable to a local church. A group of saved persons, however small, who meet in Christ's name and recognize His Presence, form a true cell in His body and enjoy the full power and authority of Christ Himself.

Because this is true the whole Christian psychology should be tuned to Christ and the Church. Every worshiper should keep before him the thought of Christ and His Church. However humble the external circumstances, if Christ is present the place is a holy temple and every believer a priest before the altar. Each single cell is an organic part of the larger body and is joined to the whole and to the Lord who indwells it by the life of the inliving Spirit.

A sense of the unity of the Church should

dictate our attitude toward it and shape the polity of the local assembly. Constant emphasis should be laid upon the fact that the local church is one indivisible organization and that there can be no independent "brotherhood" or "youth church" or "children's church" operating apart from the life and order of the whole. Departments within the church may seem to be necessary and may actually make for smoother functioning, especially where the church is a large one; but when any department begins to think of itself as a thing apart, unrelated to the local body, it becomes a cancer on the church's life and leads to its final destruction.

A multitude of religious organizations has grown up in recent times, most of them dedicated to one specific spiritual task. Among these we may list Bible societies, Bible schools and various business and professional groups bearing the name Christian. Undoubtedly many of these are good and useful agents through which the Church may work, but they must never be allowed to substitute for the Church. They are handmaids only; they can never take the place of the true mistress.

When all has been said, it is still true that the most perfect expression of God's will on earth will be found in the local church, whose members meet at stated times and places to worship the Lord and commune with each other and then go out to serve their generation after the manner laid down in the Scriptures.

CHAPTER

18

We Need Deliverance from Carnal Fear

Carnal fear may take either of two opposite directions. It may make us afraid to do what we know we should do, or afraid not to do what we have reason to think people expect us to do. Courage lies somewhere between these two extremes.

There is a foolish consistency which brings us into bondage to the consciences of other people. Our Christian testimony has created a certain expectation in the minds of our friends, and rather than jeopardize our standing with them we dutifully act in accordance with their expectation even though we have no inward conviction on the matter. We are simply afraid not to do what people expect of us. We cannot face our public after we have failed to do what we know they expected us to do.

This morality by public pressure is not pure morality at all. At best it is a timid righteousness of doubtful parentage; at worst it is the child of weakness and fear. A free Christian should act from within with a total disregard for the opinions of others. If a course is right he should take it because it is right, not because he is afraid not to take it. And if it is wrong he should avoid it, though he lose every friend, his property, his freedom and even his very life as a consequence.

Fear of the opinion of the group tends to regiment the members of denominations and churches and force them into a cookie-cutter uniformity. The desire to stand well with our own circle of religious friends destroys originality and makes imitators out of us. Various churches have their approved experiences, their shibboleths, even their accepted religious tones; these become standard for the group and are to the local fellowship what circumcision was to Israel, a ceremonial token of acceptance into the clan.

The great fault in all this is that it shifts the life motivation from within to without, from God to our fellow man. Any act done because we are afraid not to do it must take its place along with any act that is not done because we are afraid to do it. Fear, not love and faith, dictates the conduct, and whatsoever is not of faith is sin.

The way to escape this double snare is simple. Make a complete surrender to God; love Him with all your heart and love every man for His sake. Determine to obey your own convictions as they crystallize within you as a result of prayer and constant study of the Scriptures. After that you may safely ignore the expectations of your friends as well as the criticisms of your enemies. You will experience first the shocked surprise of the regimented army of lock-step believers, then their grudging admiration, and if you continue to walk the way of love and courage they will take heart from your example, throw off the bondage of fear and go forth as ransomed men and women to walk in the sweet liberty wherewith Christ has made them free.

CHAPTER
19

We Must Not Be Afraid to Look

In reading such men as Wesley and Finney one is struck with the bold way they dealt with hindrances to God's work wherever they found them. They dared to look at any work of religion, to examine the claims of any would-be prophet, and appraise them for what they were worth. They were thus able to purge out those false elements which, if allowed to remain, would soon have brought the work of God to a stop.

This is an art which very much needs to be revived in the tricky times in which we live. We now seem afraid to probe into anything that claims to be of God lest we violate the spirit of love or lay irreverent hands upon the ark.

Have we forgotten that we labor under a direct injunction to "try the spirits" and "prove all things"? Through our failure to obey this charge a hundred abuses are allowed to linger within the Church, weakening it, hindering it and throwing it open to just reproach.

The fashion now is to tolerate anything lest we gain the reputation of being intolerant. The tender-minded saints cannot bear to see Agag slain (see First Samuel 15), so they choose rather to sacrifice the health of the Church for years to come by sparing error and evil; and this they do in the name of Christian love.

We are under obligation to disturb all seats of wickedness, and where this is done out of sincere love for God and men, great good is bound to follow. No true work of God will suffer from the prayerful examination of Spirit-filled men. Timidity masquerading as love has allowed useless forms and unscriptural practices to persist in many a church till they have slowly smothered the life out of it and brought it to desolation. And many a promising work of revival has been wrecked because no one was courageous enough to stand against the abuses that entered to destroy it.

We must not be afraid to inquire. The difficulty, of course, is to do this in a Christian spirit. It is hard to find fault without being a faultfinder or to criticize without being censorious. But we have it to do if we hope to keep the work of God pure in a day of iniquity.

CHAPTER

20

Integration or Repudiation?

The world seems to possess a real genius for being wrong, even the educated world. We might just let that pass and go fishing except that we Christians happen to be living in the world and we have an obligation to be right—in everything, all of the time. We cannot afford to be wrong.

I can see how a right man might live in a wrong world and not be much affected by it except that the world will not let him alone. It wants to educate him. It is forever coming up with some new idea which, by the way, is usually an old idea dusted off and shined up for the occasion, and demanding that everyone, including the said right man, conform on pain of deep-seated frustration or a horrible complex of some kind.

Society, being fluid, usually moves like the wind, going all out in one direction until the novelty wears off or there is a war or a depression. Then the breeze sets another way and everyone is supposed to go along with it without asking too many questions, though this constant change of direction should certainly cause the thoughtful soul to wonder whether anyone really knows what all the excitement is about after all.

Right now the zephyrs are blowing in the direction of social integration, sometimes also called social adjustment. According to this notion society is possessed of a norm, a sort of best-of-all-possible model after which we must all pattern ourselves if we want to escape sundry psychosomatic disorders and emotional upsets. The only safety for any of us is in becoming so well adjusted to the other members of society as to reduce the nervous and mental friction to a minimum. Education therefore should first of all teach adjustment to society. Whatever people happen to be interested in at the moment must be accepted as normal, and any nonconformity on the part of anyone is bad for the individual and harmful to everybody. Our highest ambition should be to become integrated to the mass, to lose our moral individuality in the whole.

However absurd this may appear when thus stated baldly it is nevertheless a fair description of the most popular brand of philosophy now engaging the attention of society. So many and so efficient are the media of mass communication that when the Brahmans of the educational world decide that it is time for the wind to change, the commonalty quickly get the drift and swing obediently into the breeze. Anyone who resists is a killjoy and a spoilsport, to say nothing of being old-fashioned and dogmatic.

Well, if to escape the charge of being dogmatic I must accept the changing dogmas of the masses, then I am willing to be known as a dogmatist and no holds barred. We who call ourselves Christians are supposed to be a people apart. We claim to have repudiated the wisdom of this world and adopted the wisdom of the cross as the guide of our lives. We have thrown in our lot with that One who while He lived on earth was the most unadjusted of the sons of men. He would not be integrated into society. He stood above it and condemned it by withdrawing from it even while dying for it. Die for it He would, but surrender to it He would not.

The wisdom of the cross is repudiation of the world's "norm." Christ, not society, becomes the pattern of the Christian life. The believer seeks adjustment, not to the world, but to the will of God, and just to the degree that he is integrated into the heart of Christ is he out of adjustment with fallen human society. The Christian sees the world as a sinking ship from which he escapes not by integration but by abandonment.

A new moral power will flow back into the Church when we stop preaching social adjustment and begin to preach social repudiation and cross carrying. Modern Christians hope to save the world by being like it, but it will never work. The Church's power over the world springs out of her unlikeness to it, never from her integration into it.

CHAPTER
21

On Provocation

The word provoke means to stir up, to arouse. It may be used in a good sense but is so used only rarely. Mostly it refers to the act of making people angry by some real or supposed affront.

We have all noticed how quick many people are to excuse themselves for some outburst by pleading that they were provoked to it. Thus their own wrongdoing is laid to others. What is overlooked in this neat trick of self-exoneration is that provocation cannot stir up what is not there. It never adds anything to the human heart; it merely brings out what is already present. It does not change the character; it simply reveals it.

What a man does under provocation is what he is. The mud must be at the bottom of the pool or it cannot be stirred up. You cannot roil pure water. Provocation does not create the moral muck; it brings it to the surface. No more.

A holy man cannot be provoked to unholy acts. A pure-hearted man may be stirred to action by any of several stimuli, but the action will always accord with the purity of his heart. "Love is not easily provoked," said Paul, and the word "easily" is generally held to be an interpolation. "Love is not provoked," say the majority of translations, though some put the word irritated for provoked, making it read, "Love is not irritable." But granted that love may be provoked, it can never be provoked to any act incompatible with itself. If it is stirred to action the action will be in accord with its own nature. Love can never be anything but love.

It may bring some kind of cheap consolation to the man who has just lost his temper or let himself go in a display of bad disposition to consider that he was provoked to it by the act of another, but if he values his soul he will not thus excuse himself. Honesty will compel him to admit that he had a bad disposition to start with and the provocation merely brought it to the surface. The fault is his own, not that of the one who exposed it.

One thing yet should be added: The New Testament warns that those who incite others to evil acts will themselves be brought to stern justice. The devil tempted Christ but could not persuade Him to do wrong. Christ could not be stirred to evil because there was no evil in Him to stir. Satan's efforts were wasted, and no harm was done; nevertheless he must yet face the terror of God's judgment for his unholy attempt. Whoever puts a stumbling block in the path of the Christian will receive just punishment whether or not he succeeds in causing him to fall. Before the pool can be muddied the muck must indeed be at the bottom, but the hot anger of God will move against the one who delights to stir it up.

CHAPTER

22

Faith or Imagination

When considering the resurrection of Christ and the promised future resurrection of the redeemed, we may at times be disturbed by a sense of unreality about the whole thing. We just cannot picture it. The thought of it is so completely unlike anything that has occurred in our experience that our minds cannot find a definite place to light; so they flutter over the idea like a bird over unfamiliar terrain.

No doubt this bothers many of God's people not a little. They fear that the mental uncertainty they feel is a proof of unbelief and wonder whether they actually believe in the resurrection of the body as taught in the New Testament and repeated in the Creed. I believe these fears are groundless. Here's why:

These "fearful saints" are confusing two things which are wholly unlike each other, that is, they are confusing faith and imagination. Faith is confidence in the character of a moral being which takes the word of that being as completely trustworthy and rests in it without question. Imagination is the power to visualize, to create in the mind a picture of things unseen. We may have either one without the other. The two are not identical and are indeed only distantly related.

A soldier has been overseas two or three years and is now on his way home. As he gets closer to his native shores anticipation mounts in his heart. He visualizes the joyous meeting soon to take place. He pictures his mother, his sister, his wife, and he smiles as he thinks of how much his little son may have grown since he saw him last. The whole scene is before him as he dreams of the long-awaited reunion. Intelligence dictates a slight difference in the appearance of his loved ones. He knows they will have changed, and he tries to adjust his mental image accordingly. He thus visualizes an event which has not yet occurred by drawing on past experience.

It is right here that thought breaks down when it comes to the resurrection. We have no experience to guide us. When Christ rose from the dead He did what no one had ever done before. We cannot imagine how He accomplished the miracle. We are not even sure exactly what wonderful thing happened there in the silence of Joseph's new tomb. That He came forth, alive forevermore, has been the firmly settled faith of the Church from the beginning. How He accomplished it is a secret locked in the mind of God. We should remember the wise admonition of John Wesley: "Let us not doubt a fact because we do not know how it was accomplished." The resurrection of Christ is a fact. More than that we need not know.

Our own future resurrection is even harder to visualize. To paint a mental picture of our death is not so difficult because it has been our experience that everyone goes out that way.

> Thou knowest 'tis common,—all that live
> must die,
> Passing through nature to eternity.

The mind can visualize our departure from this earth because it has something to guide it in forming its mental picture, but the resurrection affords it no familiar stuff with which to work. And here is where anxiety and self-reproach enter. Because we cannot visualize it we are afraid that we do not believe it.

The hope of the resurrection is a matter of pure faith. It rests upon the character of God and draws its comfort from the knowledge that God cannot lie nor deceive nor change. He has promised that all who sleep in Jesus shall be brought again from their graves to meet the Lord in the air and be with Him forever. The New Testament is filled with this joyful expectation. How God will bring it all to pass is not for us to know. We are not called to understand, but to believe.

Though a detailed knowledge of the mysterious ways of God in accomplishing the resurrection were possible for us, I wonder if we would be any better off for it. We honor God more by believing Him to do the impossible. And after all, nothing is impossible with God.

CHAPTER
23

Are We Having a Revival of True Religion? Part I

That there has been a large-scale return to religion in the Western world, and more particularly in the United States, is too evident to need much proof. Religion is in vogue again. It is now considered smart to be religious.

This movement toward religion set in about the time of the Second World War and has continued ever since, in violent contrast to the attitudes that prevailed after the First World War. Civilized men came out of that first world struggle bitter, cynical, disillusioned and thoroughly angry with God. False prophets, in and out of the pulpits, had led people to believe that the race had progressed so far in the direction of universal brotherhood that war had become impossible. The arguments they advanced in support of their belief were too fragile to stand up under the battering of facts, but faith in peace and brotherhood had come on the world like a Yo-yo epidemic and everybody that was anybody was playing with it. The only voices that sounded a discordant note in the universal chorus of peace were those of the Fundamentalists who were ignored completely as being unlearned, reactionary and 200 years behind the times. So cheerfully singing a lullaby of "Peace, peace," the world plunged into a blood bath the like of which had not been known or imagined up to that time. What the people did not believe could happen did happen before their eyes. Like Cain of old, the world was exceeding wroth and its countenance fell. God had let the human race down. Religion was a fraud. Piety was hypocrisy and prayer a throwback to the jungle. They would have no more of that.

An embittered world took revenge on the hope that had failed it by debunking everything formerly considered sacred. The popular writers of the period gleefully exposed the weaknesses of everyone in history that had enjoyed a reputation for godliness or even plain decency. The Puritans were shown to be hard, cruel men who hated the human race; the Pilgrim Fathers were tried and found guilty of downright hypocrisy. Washington was a whisky sot and Lincoln a neurotic who loved off-color stories and used religion only as a convenient cloak. And so it was with everyone and everything else associated with religion.

Hardly anyone of any prominence in literary and philosophical circles believed in God. A "new era" was just ahead when the "new masses" would rise up, throw off the yoke of religion and establish a "new republic," a Marxian utopia having most of the characteristics of the Biblical millennium, but with one important difference: this man-made golden age would have no place for God or Christ or the Bible. Or if there were to be a Bible it would not be the Hebrew-Christian book given by divine inspiration, but a humanistic anthology composed of select passages from writers of the stripe of Lucretius, Rosseau and Shaw, compiled very likely by Henry Mencken or H.G. Wells.

A new dream of peace and brotherhood had come to the world, rising this time not from misplaced religious faith, as the previous dream had done, but from a thoroughly mundane secularism that would have no part of God or religion. The spiritual atmosphere between the two wars was materialistic, skeptical and self-confident. The prevailing ideology was a watered-down and disguised communism. The Commies were romping all over the White House lawn, lecturing in our universities and writing for our best magazines. The prevailing mood was humanistic. The motivating philosophies varied from each other in minor details, but they were all "one world" philosophies. This world was all that mattered. Anything beyond it was speculative and unproved. Faith in a world above was mere wishful thinking and could actually slow down human progress by lulling men into inactivity.

In such a soul state the civilized world moved into the unspeakable horrors of World War 2. Then the wholesale murder of civilian populations, the incredible iniquities of the Nazis, the shocking collapse of trust among the nations of the earth, the monstrous violations of the spirit of brotherhood, the inhumanity of man to man, the triumph of perfidy, the near ending of civilization, and finally the appearance of weapons potentially capable of bringing a flaming end to the human race itself—all this quite literally scared people into a return to religion. The humanists had failed. The starry-eyed faith in man's ability to find his way alone was bombed and burned out of people's hearts. The world began to look around for God.

So came about the return to religion. The mid-fifties finds the pendulum swung to the opposite extreme from where it was in the mid-twenties. Religion is back in style again. People can now talk about their faith without apology. It is intellectually respectable again to believe in God. The religious motif is back in the literary and entertainment world once more. Just everybody and anybody is willing to come forward and say, "This I believe." And no one acts embarrassed or changes the subject. Religion is back in fashion.

The fact cannot be disputed.

CHAPTER

24

Are We Having a Revival of True Religion? Part II

Religion is again legal in America. It is no longer necessary to whisper about it behind our hand. It is back in season.

The secular press, which of course is always quick to sense trends and give the public what it wants, has found that religion is news. A sufficiently large number of those who buy newspapers and magazines are interested enough in religion to make it profitable to print increasingly generous amounts of religious copy. Religious books are among the best sellers. Prominent people are telling the world what they believe. Religion is woven into sports, politics, the theatre. It is frequently a part of night club chatter, and the radio and TV comedian has learned that a serious word about prayer and church going at the end of his routine will please most of his listeners.

That is not all. The three major religious faiths in the United States are spending huge sums in advertising and are competing for attention in the press and on the radio. So many churches and other religious structures are being built these days that the building industry, which once considered such things something of a dead weight, is pretty well steamed up about the whole thing and is now quite eager to have the religious trade. Church membership is growing out of all proportion to the growth of the population. Converts to one or another religion are being sought on every level of society and among all classes and age groups. We have zealous work going on among children and young people. We are using sound trucks, radio, television, streetcar cards, billboards, neon signs, messages in bottles and on balloons. We are using trained horses, trained dogs, trained canaries, ventriloquists, magicians and drama to stir up religious interest. Innumerable professional guilds, industrial clubs and business men's and women's committees have sprung up to provide spiritual fellowship for religious-minded persons engaged in the various pursuits of life. Religious songs are in the repertoire of many professional entertainers. Religion is being plugged by night club entertainers, prize fighters, movie stars, and by at least one incarcerated gangster who has up to this time shown no sorrow for his way of life and no evidence of repentance. Religion, if you please, is now big business.

Unquestionably much of the religious activity of the day is good and in keeping with the ways of God as revealed in the Scriptures. Conversely, a lot of it is worldly, carnal and wholly indefensible in the light of revealed truth. Everything I have stated here is true and is too well known to be disputed. The facts are before us. The questions that are troubling many serious-minded persons are these: Do these facts add up to a revival of true religion? Is this that? Is what we are growing so luxuriantly wheat or tares? or is it a mixture of both? If it is both, do we see a great field of wheat with a few tares? or a wilderness of tares with an occasional stalk of wheat? Is this new interest in religion a result of the operation of the Holy Spirit? Is this resurgence of religious zeal on a level with that which swept over Germany in the days of Luther, or over England in the time of Wesley? In short, is this New Testament Christianity?

To some people these questions are meaningless, and if they bothered to notice them almost every answer would be "yes." The secular press greets the current return to religion with starry-eyed optimism, and even the religious press either hails it as a triumph for the Kingdom of God or ventures no appraisal at all. I think it may be conservatively stated that the great majority of our religious leaders accept the present swing toward religion as a genuine expression of a deep human longing after God and righteousness and want to encourage it all they can. Though some of them privately deplore many things associated with this religious movement they are too cautious to speak out. Their position is: It may not be perfect but it is better than nothing. So let the good work go on.

My purpose in these six chapters is to appraise the religious phenomenon which I have called (appropriating a phrase from Dr. Link) "a return to religion." Knowing that my words will be about as welcome to many persons as were the words of Micaiah at the court of King Ahab, I yet venture to say that I am not too happy about the way things are going. While I thank God reverently for any shreds of true Christianity that may be left among us, I am far from encouraged by what my eyes behold in the religious world. I'll give my reasons in the remaining four chapters in this series.

CHAPTER

25

Are We Having a Revival of True Religion? Part III

At this point it would appear necessary to define terms. Before communication can be established between writer and reader there must be a common understanding as to the meaning of words. I'll explain what I mean by "true religion."

To the convinced Christian there can be but one true religion. The half-converted may shy away from the bigotry and intolerance which he fears lie in an exclusive devotion to Christianity, but the wholly converted will have no such apprehensions. To him Christ is all in all and the faith of Christ is God's last word to mankind. To him there is but one God, the Father; one Lord and Savior, one faith, one baptism, one body, one Spirit, one fold and one Shepherd. To him there is none other name under heaven given among men whereby we must be saved. For him Christ is the only way, the only truth and the only life. For him Christ is the only wisdom, the only righteousness, the only sanctification and the only redemption. He knows that his convictions will bring him into disrepute with the so-called liberals, and he knows he will be branded as narrow and "17th century" in his thinking. But he is willing to bear the stigma. What he has seen and heard and experienced precludes any possibility of compromise. He must be true to the heavenly vision.

When, therefore, I ask the question, "Are we having a revival of true religion?" I have only one religion in mind. I mean the faith of the New Testament as held and experienced by the Fathers. I mean that religion of which Moses and all the prophets did write, that religion which originated in the heart of God the Father, was made effectual through the hard dying and triumphant resurrection of God the Son and is vitalized and propagated among men by God the Holy Spirit. Of this religion the Hebrew and Christian Scriptures are the source book, the first and last word, to which we dare add nothing and from which we dare take nothing away.

If the reader does not agree with my definition of true religion, then communication between us breaks down. There is no point in using words which mean one thing to me and another to the reader. Unless we agree to let the Scriptures tell us what true religion is, there is no way for us to find out. Each man is thrown back into the depths of his own dark ignorance and must feel his way along the steep sides of the abyss from which there is no escape.

If, on the other hand, we agree to let the Word of God decide what is and is not the religion of Christ, an inspired pattern is established for us and we are saved from tragic and costly errors concerning this all-important matter.

Once this standard is acknowledged it is not too difficult to test a given doctrine or practice to determine whether it is of God or not. We have only to compare everything that professes to be New Testament Christianity with the New Testament itself. "To the law and to the testimony: if they speak not according to this word, it is because there is no light in them" (Isaiah 8:20, KJV).

Every activity now being carried on in the name of Christ must meet the last supreme test: Does it have biblical authority back of it? Is it according to the letter and the spirit of the Scripture? Is its spiritual content divinely given? That it succeeds proves nothing. That it is popular proves less. Where are the proofs of its heavenly birth? Where are its scriptural credentials? What assurance does it give that it represents the operation of the Holy Spirit in the divine plan of the ages? These questions demand satisfactory answers.

No one should object to an honest examination of his work in the pure light of Scripture. No honest man will shrink from the light, nor will he defend beliefs and practices that cannot be justified by the test of truth. Rather he will eagerly seek to build according to the pattern shown him in the mount.

> Therefore everyone who hears these words of mine and puts them into practice is like a wise man who built his house on the rock. The rain came down, the streams rose, and the winds blew and beat against the house; yet it did not fall because it had its foundation on the rock. (Matthew 7:24–25)

Are we today building on the rock? Upon the answer hangs our little all. We had better be sure.

CHAPTER

26

Are We Having a Revival of True Religion? Part IV

In an attempt to discover whether the present increase in religious interest indicates a genuine revival of biblical Christianity I propose some easy tests. First: *Is the spiritual content of current popular religion identical with or even close to that of the New Testament? Is this that?*

I do not mean to imply that a true religious revival must be free from faults. To require perfection in the work of God among fallen men would not be realistic. Though God is perfect, men are not, and God must deal with them as He finds them. The work of Christ was flawless, but the response of His followers was imperfect and full of faults. The New Testament Epistles and the seven letters of the book of Revelation reveal that the first Christians were not always models of perfection. Every reformation and revival from Pentecost to modern times has had its faults, its vagaries and excesses along with its purity and its power. All this we freely admit. We do not require perfection as a proof of the genuineness of revival.

What we do require before we will admit its authenticity is that the spirit, the temper, of a religious movement must be scriptural. The color and flavor must be that of the New Testament. The spiritual essence of the Gospels and Epistles must appear in any religious phenomenon or it is instantly disqualified and must be rejected as spurious.

By this test it is plain that the current return to religion is not a return to the faith of Christ and the apostles. The temper is not the same; the spiritual content is of another essence; the quality is not only inferior but of another kind altogether. By every spiritual test this is not that.

True, the voice is Jacob's voice. The current return to religion is ostensibly a return to the faith of Christ, for the language employed is that of the Bible. But the hands are the hands of Esau. The practice is not consonant with the testimony. The two are not only different from, they are hostile to, each other.

Except in rare and isolated instances current Christianity is not producing godliness. And where an example of true saintliness appears occasionally it will be found to be a throwback to another and more serious type of religion than that to which people have "returned" in such numbers today. My own observation has taught me that the few who are yearning to be Christlike are being forced to dissent from most of what they see around them and go it alone in their holy longing after God. Scarcely any religious activities today conduce to holiness. The hungry seeker after personal godliness must look beyond the current "revival." He'll not find much help there.

If anyone should wonder what I mean by godliness, saintliness, holiness, I'll explain. I mean a life and a heart marked by *meekness* and *humility*. The godly soul will not boast nor show off. I mean *reverence*. The godly man will never take part in any religious exercise that shows disrespect for the Deity. The cozy, cute terms now applied to God and Christ will never pass his lips. He will never join in singing religious songs that are light, humorous or irreverent. He will cultivate a spirit of complete sincerity and discuss God and religion only in grave and reverent tones.

Further, I mean *separation* from the world unto God in an all-out, irrevocable committal. The holy man will not envy the world, nor will he imitate it or seek its approval. His testimony will be, "I am crucified unto the world and the world unto me." He will not depend upon it for his enjoyments, but will look above and within for the joy that is unspeakable and full of glory.

In short, any true work of God in the churches will result in an intensified spirit of worship and an elevated appreciation of the basic Christian virtues as they are set forth in the New Testament. It will result in self-denial and cross carrying among the people. It will make men Christlike, will free them from a thousand carnal sins they did not even know were sins before. It will free them from earthly entanglements and focus their whole attention upon things above.

This is not a dreamer's view of the Christian faith. The New Testament abundantly supports what is written here. In the light of the facts, may we conclude that the current wave of religious interest is an indication that a revival is on? Obviously not. And there are other and more convincing tests to come.

CHAPTER
27

Are We Having a Revival of True Religion? Part V

Were a resurgence of the true faith of Christ to occur anywhere in the civilized world we would have every right to expect those affected by it to become more spiritual, more saintly, in the best sense of these words. The present wave of religion is having no such effect. Indeed the whole concept of saintliness is absent. The yearning to be holy can scarcely be found among the busy religionists of the day.

Christianity once set out to convert the world and ended by undergoing a reverse conversion. The world converted the Church, and after the passing of 16 centuries we are still suffering from the disgraceful surrender. Rome introduced her pagan ways into the pure stream of the Christian faith and the waters are still muddy after how many noble efforts to purify them. And that great half-Christian, half-pagan institution, the Roman Catholic Church, which took its rise at the time of that historic reverse conversion, moves on from victory to victory and continues to spread itself across the face of the whole world.

The rise of a new religious spirit in recent years is marked by disturbing similarities to that earlier "revival" under Constantine. Now as then a quasi-Christianity is achieving acceptance by compromise. It is dickering with the unregenerate world for acceptance and, as someone said recently, it is offering Christ at bargain prices to win customers. The total result is a conglomerate religious mess that cannot but make the reverent Christian sick in his heart.

Without the remotest intention to accept the authority of Christ many religious leaders nevertheless use His name as an attractive front to give them entree to the masses. Whether or not it is the fulfillment of that odd passage in Isaiah, still it reminds one of the words, "In that day seven women/ will take hold of one man/ and say, 'We will eat our own food/ and provide our own clothes;/ only let us be called by your name./ Take away our disgrace' " (Isaiah 4:1). Doctrines wholly foreign to the Scriptures are being taught in the name of Christ (as, for instance, the strange humanistic hodgepodge of Norman Vincent Peale); and His name is being pronounced over deeds as carnal and earthly as any ever performed under the sun. The "Man Upstairs" of war days is now being invoked to bring success to the selfish schemes of unregenerate men.

One movie star, after a half hour of fighting, shooting and general mayhem closes his radio show with the folksy benediction, "May the good Lord take a likin' to you." A night club gossip monger ends his broadcast with the exhortation, "And go with God." A disc jockey who broadcasts from a saloon has been known to interview religious persons on his program and to draw them out to tell of the power of prayer. A famous night club comedian publicly testifies that he became a thousand-dollar-a-week success after praying to a statue and promising to contribute generously of his income to humanitarian purposes. The sight of the Virgin and the Holy Child in a tavern window surrounded by whisky bottles is not uncommon at the Christmas season in the large cities.

The sum of all this is that religion today is not transforming the people; rather it is being transformed by the people. It is not raising the moral level of society; it is descending to society's own level and congratulating itself that it has scored a victory because society is smilingly accepting its surrender.

What too many religious leaders are overlooking is that the faith of Christ makes no concessions, accepts no compromises, allows no terms and makes no deals. Christ offers Himself to men as Lord and Savior and receives returning sinners only when they turn against themselves and come fully over on God's side. Fallen men escape the judgment of the world as Lot escaped the destruction of Sodom, by forsaking it altogether, not by getting adjusted to it.

The current vogue religion never says, "Thou shalt not;" that would be negative thinking and contrary to the best psychology. It does not command men; it smiles and cajoles and suggests and ends by letting the man have his own way. Anything goes as long as a sop is tossed to God in the form of "devotions" after the unreconstructed rebel has had his fun. God thus becomes a servant who stands ready to help in a pinch but who will not make any embarrassing demands or expect anyone to live a life much different from the customary easy life made familiar by the radio and the public press.

Undoubtedly here and there a happy exception may be found. The Holy Spirit has His few, as indeed He has always had, and their holy walk and tear-drenched prayers may yet save the day.

CHAPTER
28

Are We Having a Revival of True Religion? Part VI

In the darkest days of Israel's history God never left Himself without a witness. Even when the worship of Baal was supreme in the land there were "seven thousand" who remained true to Jehovah.

It is a matter of deep personal gratification to me that I can and do believe that there is even in these degenerate times an elect remnant which seeks to know and do the will of God at any cost. And there is a slight possibility that that remnant may be larger today than it was a few years ago. I pray that I may have underestimated the number of the truly saved and that things may be brighter than I think. But making all allowance for what may be a too low view of the matter and drawing upon all Christian hopefulness and charity, I still cannot accept the idea that we in the United States are enjoying today a revival of the true Christian faith. A widely quoted British magazine about a year ago informed the world that we in America were indeed experiencing a "religious revival amounting to a social revolution." It is hard to imagine a more erroneous report, though undoubtedly it was published in good faith. The editors made the mistake of printing encouraging rumors without checking on the truth of them.

A genuine revival would raise the moral standards of society; instead, those standards are at a dismally low level everywhere. A genuine revival would check the divorce rate and bring back the sanctity of the home; instead, the divorce rate is higher than ever and the home is becoming little more than a place to sleep and watch television. A revival of true religion would discourage crime and juvenile delinquency; instead, the crime rate is higher than at any time in our history and youthful gang wars have become major police problems in our large cities.

Were the faith of our fathers exercising a major influence in society there would be a revolution in moral values among all Christians and a change in the outlook of multitudes who, while not themselves Christians, would nevertheless feel the strong pressure of Christian ethics and ideals around them. So it was in Italy under Savonarola, in Geneva under Calvin, in Germany in the time of Luther, in the England of the Wesleys and on a smaller scale in many places where revivals have broken out in cities and communities over the past centuries.

But in America no such change is found. The present flair for religion has not made people heavenly minded; rather it has secularized religion and put its approval upon the carnal values of fallen men. It glorifies success and eagerly prints religious testimonials from big corporation tycoons, actors, athletes, politicians and very important persons of every kind regardless of their reputation or lack of one. Religion is promoted by the identical techniques used to sell cigarettes. You pray to soothe your nerves just as you smoke to regain your composure after a sharp business transaction or a tight athletic contest. Books are written by the scores to show that Jesus is a Regular Fellow and Christianity a wise use of the highest psychological laws. All the holy principles of the Sermon on the Mount are present in reverse. Not the meek are blessed, but the self-important; not they that mourn but they that smile and smile and smile. Not the poor in spirit are dear to God, but they who are accounted somebody by the secular press. Not they that hunger and thirst after righteousness are filled, but they that hunger for publicity.

If I were describing only the nonevangelical religions the whole thing would not be so shocking. The fact is that the most popular gospel groups are deeply affected with this antigospel decay. To a tragic degree evangelical Christianity is now scriptural only in name. It has a name to live but is dead.

This has been an honest effort to understand the religious situation in the present critical hour. It is not meant as a denunciation, but as an appraisal. Surely there are a few names even today who have not defiled their garments and they shall walk with God in white, for they are worthy. Possibly we are coming near to a time when those who are on the Lord's side may be forced to withdraw from the religious hodgepodge and form a company of believers that will insist upon New Testament doctrine and New Testament practice. The temple waits to be cleansed. We should pray day and night till that happy event takes place.

CHAPTER 29

No Competition

It is inherent in the nature of the religion of Christ that it cannot be promoted by competitive acts.

The essence of Christianity is selfless love. This was expressed first by our Lord in His redemptive suffering and has been expressed again and again since in every artless deed of kindness done by His followers for each other and for a suffering world. The essence of competition is self-love. Men compete to gain something for themselves, and in doing so they must of necessity cause someone else to lose what they gain. From this we gather that the two spirits are opposed to each other. We cannot be selfish and selfless at the same time.

Nothing spiritual can be gained in competition. The very idea of struggling with another for some eternal treasure of the soul is unthinkable. John D. Rockefeller used to enjoy throwing a handful of shiny new dimes to a crowd of children and watching them scramble after them, each one struggling to grab as many as possible. The gifts and graces of God are not thus obtained. Each one of God's children can have all of Him and no one need receive less because another receives an abundance.

When two men step into a prize ring they know that only one can win, and whoever wins can do so only by forcing the other to lose. When five men line up on the track for a race they know that only one can come in first. Four men must lose that one may win. It is not so in the kingdom of God. Christians do not run against each other. All can win the race. Paul likens a Christian to a fighter, but the Christian's fight is not with other Christians. Each one can win and no one need lose. The man of faith fights against the devil, the flesh and the world. He wins as they lose; but he never wins anything truly spiritual in competition with a fellow believer. In the nature of things he cannot. To think so is to entertain an absurdity.

Whatever religious activity is, or even can be, promoted in a spirit of competition is of the flesh and must perish with the flesh; in the day of Christ nothing will remain but self-reproach and disappointment. Yet there are forms of religious promotion that lend themselves to selfish uses. The earthly scaffoldings of the Christian faith are often constructed from motives no higher than jealousy and personal ambition. The eternal part is above the reach of carnal men; the temporal elements are subject to the manipulations of ambitious leaders who seek glory for themselves. And verily they have their reward.

Circumstances being what they are the Christian minister is the one most tempted to carry on competitive religious activity. Even where his self-respect and good taste will not allow him to engage in an obvious race for numbers or publicity or fame he may yet harbor the spirit of envy within his heart and so be as guilty as the coarser and less inhibited bellwether who openly seeks to excel. He can get deliverance from the spirit of religious rivalry by going straight to God and having an understanding about the whole thing. Let him humble himself in the presence of God and in all earnestness pray somewhat like this:

> Dear Lord, I refuse henceforth to compete with any of Thy servants. They have congregations larger than mine. So be it. I rejoice in their success. They have greater gifts. Very well. That is not in their power nor in mine. I am humbly grateful for their greater gifts and my smaller ones. I only pray that I may use to Thy glory such modest gifts as I possess. I will not compare myself with any, nor try to build up my self-esteem by noting where I may excel one or another in Thy holy work. I herewith make a blanket disavowal of all intrinsic worth. I am but an unprofitable servant. I gladly go to the foot of the class

> and own myself the least of Thy people. If I err in my self-judgment and actually underestimate myself I do not want to know it. I purpose to pray for others and to rejoice in their prosperity as if it were my own. And indeed it is my own if it is Thine own, for what is Thine is mine, and while one plants and another waters it is Thou alone that giveth the increase.

The man who walks according to the spirit of this prayer will find himself free from all envy and all rivalry and will be at liberty to serve God in the simplicity and power of the Holy Ghost. Such a man will build with gold and silver and precious stones and will escape the tragedy of discovering too late that he has built of wood, hay and stubble.

CHAPTER

30

We Must Think Right If We Would Be Right

What we think about when we are free to think about what we will—that is what we are or will soon become.

The Bible has a great deal to say about our thoughts; current evangelicalism has practically nothing to say about them. The reason the Bible says so much is that our thoughts are so vitally important to us; the reason evangelicalism says so little is that we are overreacting from the "thought" cults, such as New Thought, Unity, Christian Science and their like. These cults make our thoughts to be very nearly everything and we counter by making them very nearly nothing. Both positions are wrong.

Our voluntary thoughts not only reveal what we are, they predict what we will become. Except for that conduct which springs from our basic natural instincts, all conscious behavior is preceded by and arises out of our thoughts. The will can become a servant of the thoughts, and to a large degree even our emotions follow our thinking. "The more I think about it the madder I get" is the way the average man states it, and in so doing not only reports accurately on his own mental processes but pays as well an unconscious tribute to the power of thought. Thinking stirs feeling and feeling triggers action. That is the way we are made and we may as well accept it.

The psalms and prophets contain numerous references to the power of right thinking to raise religious feeling and incite to right conduct. "I thought on my ways, and turned my feet unto thy testimonies." "While I was musing the fire burned: then spake I with my tongue." Over and over the Old Testament writers exhort us to get quiet and think about high and holy things as a preliminary to amendment of life or a good deed or a courageous act.

The Old Testament is not alone in its respect for the God-given power of human thought. Christ taught that men defile themselves by evil thinking and even went so far as to equate a thought with an act: "Anyone who looks at a woman lustfully has already committed adultery with her in his heart" (Matthew 5:28). Paul recited a list of shining virtues and commanded, "Think on these things" (Philippians 4:8).

These quotations are but four out of hundreds that could be cited from the Scriptures. Thinking about God and holy things creates a moral climate favorable to the growth of faith and love and humility and reverence. We cannot by thinking regenerate our hearts, nor take our sins away nor change the leopard's spots. Neither can we by thinking add one cubit to our stature or make evil good or darkness light. So to teach is to misrepresent a scriptural truth and to use it to our own undoing. But we can by Spirit-inspired thinking help to make our minds pure sanctuaries in which God will be pleased to dwell.

I referred in a previous paragraph to "our voluntary thoughts" and I used the words advisedly. In our journey through this evil and hostile world many thoughts will be forced upon us which we do not like and for which we have no moral sympathy. The necessity to make a living may compel us for days on end to entertain thoughts in no sense elevating. Ordinary awareness of the doings of our fellow men will bring thoughts repugnant to our Christian souls. These need affect us but little. For them we are not responsible and they may pass through our minds like a bird through the air, without leaving a trace. They have no lasting effect upon us because they are not our own. They are unwelcome intruders for which we have no love and which we get rid of as quickly as possible.

Anyone who wishes to check on his true spiritual condition may do so by noting what his voluntary thoughts have been over the last hours or days. What has he thought about when free to think of what he pleased? Toward what has his inner heart turned when it was free to turn where it would? When the bird of thought was let go did it fly out like the raven to settle upon floating carcasses or did it like the dove circle and return again to the ark of God? Such a test is easy to run, and if we are honest with ourselves we can discover not only what we are but what we are going to become. We'll soon be the sum of our voluntary thoughts.

While our thoughts stir our feelings, and thus strongly influence our wills, it is yet true that the will can be and should be master of our thoughts. Every normal person can determine what he will think about. Of course the troubled or tempted man may find his thoughts somewhat difficult to control and even while he is concentrating upon a worthy object, wild and fugitive thoughts may play over his mind like heat lightning on a summer evening. These are likely to be more bothersome than harmful and in the long run do not make much difference one way or another.

The best way to control our thoughts is to offer the mind to God in complete surrender. The Holy Spirit will accept it and take control of it immediately. Then it will be relatively easy to think on spiritual things, especially if we train our thoughts by long periods of daily prayer. Long practice in the art of mental prayer (that is, talking to God inwardly as we work or travel) will help to form the habit of holy thought.

The best way of all is to "let this mind be in you, which was also in Christ Jesus." For to have the mind of Christ is to have good and pure thoughts always.

CHAPTER

31

Not Moses, But Abraham

The Christian's spiritual progenitor is not Moses but Abraham.

The great doctrine of faith takes us back to Abraham and thus antedates the Law of Moses by 430 years. This is the argument of Paul in Galatians 3:15–18 and Romans 4:9–16.

There is a mistaken notion abroad that in the Old Testament salvation came by obedience to the Law, while in the New Testament it comes by faith. The truth is that since the beginning of the world no one was ever saved in any way other than by grace through faith.

"The law was given by Moses, but grace and truth came by Jesus Christ." But grace and truth came by Jesus Christ long before the incarnation. When God slew those beasts (presumably lambs) and gave the skins to Adam and Eve for clothing He was telling them in symbolic language that the redemption of the race would be by the merit of innocent life laid down. Not by law but by atonement would they and their descendants be ransomed from the Fall.

This idea was never wholly lost to mankind. When the Law was given it was accompanied by a system of sin offerings and atoning sacrifices leading straight to the Savior who was to come. When John pointed to Jesus and exclaimed, "Behold the Lamb of God, which taketh away the sin of the world," he was identifying Christ with all the sacrificial lambs that had been offered for sin from the time of Abel to the appearance of Emmanuel.

The idea creeps into much evangelical teaching that the Old Testament is a book of justice and judgment without a ray of mercy or grace or love to lighten the darkness, whereas the New Testament is filled with mercy and forgiveness. The truth is that mercy and justice, love and judgment are found in both the Old and the New Testament in about equal proportion. Not two Gods but one wrote the Bible and the unity of His perfect character reveals itself in all parts of the Scriptures.

It may come as a surprise to some to learn that there is as much about mercy in the Old Testament as in the New, but such is actually the case. Grace is found throughout the Old Testament, and love also is found there in abundance. Justification by faith is an Old Testament doctrine. It was first associated with Abraham, appeared later in the writings of David and Habakkuk and was shown by Paul to be one of the most vital doctrines of the New Testament. Thus the organic unity of the Bible is confirmed.

It is a heartening thought that no one ever had or can have any advantage over another in his search for God. No matter what the dispensation or the circumstances, everyone who came to God came by faith. Those of ancient times looked forward to the cross and those of later times looked and must look back to it. Everyone and anyone may find forgiveness and cleansing through the grace of our Lord Jesus Christ, and any progress in the knowledge of God, any growth in spiritual stature must come the same way. Our spiritual ancestor is Abraham whose faith pleased God, brought an imputation of righteousness and made him the father of the faithful.

We Christians are the sons of faith and the heirs of liberty. Let us stand fast therefore in the liberty wherewith Christ has made us free.

CHAPTER

32

The Value of a Good Home

The oldest institution in the world is the home. It had its beginning in the garden which the Lord God planted eastward in Eden, where also He placed the man and the woman whom He created.

Under such ideal conditions began the home, that sacred unit of human society which through the long centuries has gathered round its head like a coronet such riches of beautiful associations and undying memories.

Consider the home. From time immemorial it has been the focal point around which our kindest thoughts gather, a refuge for the troubled, a harbor for the storm-tossed, a resting place to which we may return when weary and oppressed by a world that has been too much for us. However humble its furnishings, however modest its size, there is always room there for the heart, its richest and its most beautiful appointment.

So perverse is human nature, so wayward the

soul, that we may come to accept our childhood home as a matter of course and forget for a time what a treasure it was. But though we have strayed far from its hallowed precincts the time is sure to come when we remember it again with tender yearnings and regrets.

Let illness visit us or some heavy blow fall upon us to shake our confidence and stagger our minds: then in a flash we will remember. The heart will return home again like a dove to her window. Then will the loved faces smile once more and the voices that have been so long silent will be heard as plain as in the days of yore. In a moment the years roll back and the members of the little family group from which we have been separated so long by the miles and the years laugh together again. We recognize each friendly face, to us still young and still beautiful; we hear our nickname that we had all but forgotten and it is sweet and strange to hear it in our inner ear after the passing of the years. We know then, and confess in a rush of feeling, how precious was the time spent at home with our own people in peace before the grown-up lust for treasure or fame had lured us out into the wide world.

Impressions gained in childhood have greater power to shape our lives than anything we may learn in later years. Sometimes we are permitted to see how deeply men are affected by that first preschool education gained as it were by accident in their childhood home. That elderly man who came to our shores while still a child and who has spoken the English language for the better part of his lifetime lies down for his last sleep. Before his voice is lost in death he whispers a final prayer to his God and Father—not in the language of his adult years but in that of his motherland, first heard in the old home across the sea in the country of his birth. Life's beginnings return at its ending.

It is vitally important that our homes be preserved. A nation is only as strong as its homes. No government can substitute for the ministrations of the family. Federal agencies cannot love and cuddle the baby, not kiss his bruised knee or hear his prayer at the close of the day. Fathers and mothers make homes; nothing else can. And whether our American homes produce delinquents or upright citizens will depend altogether upon what kind of fathers and mothers preside in those homes.

If the home is the oldest institution on earth the Church is the loftiest, and historically there has always been a close relationship between the two. The family that stays close to the church is the one most likely to hold together. Churchgoing parents make churchgoing children, and while there may be an occasional exception, boys and girls brought up in Christian homes tend strongly to be good and law-abiding adults. The armies of crime do not draw their recruits from the church or Sunday school.

Police and juvenile authorities agree that the best guarantee against moral delinquency among young people is a good religious training. The example of serious-minded God-fearing persons is a tremendous power for good. Young people who have the blessing of association with earnest Christians in church and in the home have a powerful advantage over those who are reared away from the church.

The church cannot save the soul; but it can and does serve as an effective school of good living. In addition to the saving gospel which sounds forth from the pulpits of our true Christian churches, there is heard also instruction in righteousness, the value of honesty, purity and truthfulness and the superiority of the homely virtues. These things are treasures above rubies. No child should be deprived of the advantage they bring.

Parents who desire the best for their children should not overlook their spiritual nurture. To such parents we offer the following suggestions: Start taking your children to a good church regularly. Help them to get acquainted with others of their own ages within the fellowship of the church. Get them into the Sunday school, and then back up these efforts with family Bible reading. Above all, put your trust in Jesus Christ and set a good example in the home. You'll never regret that you did.

CHAPTER
33

Why We Are Lukewarm about Christ's Return

Shortly after the close of the First World War, I heard a great Southern preacher say that he feared the intense interest in prophecy current at that time would result in a dying out of the blessed hope when events had proved the excited interpreters wrong.

The man was a prophet, or at least a remarkably shrewd student of human nature, for exactly what he predicted has come to pass. The hope of Christ's coming is today all but dead among evangelicals.

I do not mean that Bible Christians have given up the doctrine of the second advent. By no means. There has been, as every informed person knows, an adjustment among some of the lesser tenets of our prophetic credo, but the vast majority of evangelicals continue to hold to the belief that Jesus Christ will sometime actually come back to the earth in person. The ultimate triumph of Christ is accepted as one of the unshakable doctrines of Holy Scripture.

It is true that in some quarters the prophecies of the Bible are occasionally expounded. This is especially so among Hebrew Christians who, for reasons well understood, seem to feel closer to the prophets of the Old Testament than do Gentile believers. Their love for their own people naturally leads them to grasp at every hope of the conversion and ultimate restoration of Israel. To many of them the return of Christ represents a quick and happy solution of the "Jewish problem." The long centuries of wandering will end when He comes and God will at that time "restore again the kingdom to Israel." We dare not allow our deep love for our Hebrew Christian brethren to blind us to the obvious political implications of this aspect of their Messianic hope. We do not blame them for this. We merely call attention to it.

Yet the return of Christ as a blessed hope is, as I said above, all but dead among us. The truth touching the second advent, where it is presented today, is for the most part either academic or political. The joyful personal element is altogether missing. Where are they who

> Yearn for the sign, O Christ, of Thy
> fulfilling,
> Faint for the flaming of Thine advent feet?

The longing to see Christ that burned in the breasts of those first Christians seems to have burned itself out. All we have left are the ashes. It is precisely the "yearning" and the "fainting" for the return of Christ that has distinguished the personal hope from the theological one. Mere acquaintance with correct doctrine is a poor substitute for Christ and familarity with New Testament eschatology will never take the place of a love-inflamed desire to look on His face.

If the tender yearning is gone from the advent hope today there must be a reason for it; and I think I know what it is, or what they are, for there are a number of them. One is simply that popular Fundamentalist theology has emphasized the utility of the cross rather than the beauty of the One who died on it. The saved man's relation to Christ has been made contractual instead of personal. The "work" of Christ has been stressed until it has eclipsed the person of Christ. Substitution has been allowed to supersede identification. What He *did for me* seems to be more important than what He *is to me*. Redemption is seen as an across-the-counter transaction which we "accept," and the whole thing lacks emotional content. We must love someone very much to stay awake and long for his coming, and that may explain the absence of power in the advent hope even among those who still believe in it.

Another reason for the absence of real yearning for Christ's return is that Christians are so comfortable in this world that they have little desire to leave it. For those leaders who set the pace of religion and determine its content and quality, Christianity has become of late remarkably lucrative. The streets of gold do not have too great an appeal for those who find it so easy to pile up gold and silver in the service of the Lord here on earth. We all want to reserve the hope of heaven as a kind of insurance against the day of death, but as long as we are healthy and comfortable, why change a familiar good for something about which we know very little actually? So reasons the carnal mind, and so subtly that we are scarcely aware of it.

Again, in these times religion has become jolly good fun right here in this present world, and what's the hurry about heaven anyway? Christianity, contrary to what some had thought, is another and higher form of entertainment. Christ has done all the suffering. He has shed all the tears and carried all the crosses; we have but to enjoy the benefits of His heartbreak in the form of religious pleasures modeled after the world but carried on in the name of Jesus. So say the same people who claim to believe in Christ's second coming.

History reveals that times of suffering for the Church have also been times of looking upward. Tribulation has always sobered God's people and encouraged them to look for and yearn after the return of their Lord. Our present preoccupation with this world may be a warning of bitter days to come. God will wean us from the earth some way—the easy way if possible, the hard way if necessary. It is up to us.

CHAPTER

34

On Omitting That Third Stanza

One of the commonest expressions heard in the public worship service is the leader's directive, "Sing the first, second and last verses;" or, "Omit the third verse, please."

Now, we'll overlook the fact that the director obviously means *stanza* and not *verse*. We are all so prone to inaccuracies of speech that it does not become any of us to be too hard on the rest of us, though it would seem that any man who accepts a position that places him before the public should inform himself on matters with which that position requires that he be familiar.

I suppose it is not of vast importance that the third stanza is so often omitted in the singing of a hymn, but just for the record let it be said that the worshipers are deprived of the blessing of the hymn by that omission if, as is often true, the hymn develops a great Christian truth in sermonic outline. To omit a stanza is to lose one link in a golden chain and greatly to reduce the value of the whole hymn.

The significant thing, however, is not what the omission actually does, but what it suggests, viz., a nervous impatience and a desire to get the service over with. We are, for instance, singing "When I Survey the Wondrous Cross." We long to forget the big noisy world and let our hearts go out in reverent worship of that Prince of Glory who died for us, but our sad sweet longing is killed in the bud by the brisk, unemotional voice of the director ordering us to "omit the third verse." We wonder vaguely whether the brother is hungry or has to catch an early train or just why he is so anxious to get through with the hymn. Since all standard hymns have been edited to delete inferior stanzas and since any stanza of the average hymn can be sung in less than one minute ("When I Survey the Wondrous Cross" clocks at 30 seconds to the stanza, normal tempo!) and since many of our best hymns have already been shortened as much as good taste will allow, we are forced to conclude that the habit of omitting the third stanza reveals religious boredom, pure and simple, and it would do our souls good if we would admit it.

If it were only in our hymn singing that this spirit were found I would probably not have brought the matter up at all, but I find it in pretty near every department of the religious life. Not the doing of evil deeds only but the omission of good deeds weakens the soul and invites the judgments of God. The same worldly, impatient spirit that shortens a hymn also shortens our prayer time and reduces the amount we give to the Lord's work, as well as the number of services we attend each week.

There is always danger that God may intend to speak to us at a gathering of the saints, and we thwart the loving purposes of God for us by not being present at the time of visitation. A wise old deacon said to the young Evan Roberts, "Now, lad, be sure to attend every prayer meeting. God may want to bless you sometime and you will miss it because you are not present. Remember Thomas and what he missed because he wasn't there." Evan never forgot that exhortation. He never missed a prayer meeting from that day on. And it is significant that it was in a prayer meeting that God touched Evan Roberts and the great Welsh revival began.

There have been devotional writers (for example, some of the so-called "mystic" theologians) who held that sin is at bottom a negation, an absence of something, a no-thing, and that its destructive power lies right there. God, they said, is the Something, the positive Entity, and evil is the repudiation of God, the denial in thought and deed of the Eternal Something that we know to be the Lord God Almighty, Maker of heaven and earth. This would appear to be too rarefied, too one-sided a concept to account for sin as the Bible and the world know it. Yet there is more than a modicum of truth in it. How much of evil is omission! "Anyone, then, who knows the good he ought to do and doesen't do it, sins" (James 4:17).

It may be that sins of omission are the worst sins of all. Dr. R.A. Torrey said that if the first and greatest commandment is to love God with all our hearts, the greatest sin is to fail to love Him. If Torrey was correct, then the darkest sin in the world is a negation, a no-thing, something men do not do. Finney preached great sermons on the sins of omission. Every Christian has felt the sharp sting of conscience over deeds not done, and sometimes the sense of guilt is greater than for wrongs committed.

The moral man who boasts that he has never lied or cheated or harmed his fellow man may be in for a shock in the day of judgment. Not to have done a positive good is to have done evil. Not to be where we should have been is as bad as to be where we should not be. To be absent when the Lord distributes His blessings may easily prove to be a real tragedy. Not to pray when we should pray is like failing to open a letter full of good news. The loss is too great to estimate.

Let's sing the third stanza.

CHAPTER

35

Let's Face the Facts

A few days ago I heard a man speak on First Corinthians 13, the familiar love chapter of the New Testament. His message pointed up a modern heresy against which I have often warned and about which I now consider it my duty to write a few words.

The preacher was not a cultist, but an evangelical and a Fundamentalist. Undoubtedly, he would have given his right eye rather than teach false doctrine or otherwise injure the souls of his hearers. Nevertheless, I believe he was injuring them and teaching false doctrine into the bargain.

The heart of his message appeared to be that the description of love in that Corinthian chapter applies to our Lord Jesus Christ. And of course it was easy to prove that it does. "Christ suffereth long, and is kind; Christ envieth not; Christ vaunteth not Himself, is not puffed up, does not behave Himself unseemly, seeketh not His own, is not easily provoked, thinketh no evil . . . " and so to the end of the chapter.

Now, no Christian would deny that Jesus

Christ, being very God of very God, has in Himself all moral virtues in full perfection. God is love and Christ is God, so it follows that anything that can be said of love can be said also of Christ. But to make Paul's words describe Christ is to read into them a meaning Paul never intended, which of course is to introduce error into the interpretation of Scripture. And the error is not one of interpretation merely; it has practical and serious consequences in that it ignores the solemn warning of the chapter and relieves us of all obligation to seek and obtain the love of God in our own hearts.

Just what is Paul telling us in this 13th chapter of his first Corinthian epistle? That love is absolutely indispensable to the Christian life. The gift of tongues without love is so much noise. The gift of prophecy without love is of no benefit. Without love, knowledge and faith are useless. And though a man bestow all his goods to feed the poor and die at last a martyr's death, if he have not love it profits him nothing. So Paul states in the first three verses, after which he describes love and identifies it so the reader will know what kind of person he must be to escape an unprofitable, empty and deceived existence.

Paul's analysis of love is not intended to tell us what kind of being Christ is, but *what kind of person a real Christian must be*. That these virtues are all in Christ, I repeat, is the common belief of all Christians, but they were not listed in the inspired Word to teach us that. So to hold and teach is to play a shoddy trick on our own souls and on the souls of our hearers.

Perhaps a homemade illustration may help. What does "health" mean for a man? Well, it means a pulse rate of 72, a body temperature of 98.6 degrees, a blood count of 5,000 white cells and 5,000,000 red cells per cubic millimeter, a respiration rate of 20 at rest, 30 percent solids to 70 percent water body composition, and so on. Any doctor could carry this on until he had described the man of ideal health.

The 13th chapter of First Corinthians may tell us what Christ is like, but let us not forget that it also tells us what we must be like to avoid spiritual tragedy. Let us not turn our back on this critically important teaching. Without love, the kind described by Paul, my whole Christian life is a barren fig tree. It's a neat trick to apply Paul's words to Christ only; but it isn't honest and it is dangerous.

It is the Holy Spirit who sheds abroad the love of God in our hearts (Romans 5:5) and love is declared to be a fruit of the Spirit (Galatians 5:22). But if our daily lives reveal that the fruit is not there we dare not assume that it is—"because the Bible says so." The absence of love as described in First Corinthians 13 is proof of the absence of the Spirit, or at least that He is inoperative within us. That's the only honest conclusion. We can't afford to be less than candid about the whole thing.

CHAPTER

36

"What Does It Take to Thrill a Man?"

A great city newspaper came up lately with an idea that might have meaning to a lot of us Christians any time and seems to be especially appropriate around the Thanksgiving season.

Asking the question, "What does it take to thrill a man?" the editorial writer said that a man whose name is known throughout the whole world, who has received from the nations of the earth just about every honor that can be accorded to men and whose own country had elected him to the highest position it could give any of its citizens, had recently expressed himself as being "thrilled" at being permitted to sit up a few minutes in a wheel chair. That man, of course, was Dwight D. Eisenhower, and the occasion was his first time out of bed after his heart attack.

This touching incident in the life of a great man should teach us that we are likely to overlook our real blessings and fail to be thankful for them because they are small or because they appear to be trifling and ordinary. We may be grateful for life's rare mountain peaks and fail completely to see the dozens or scores of little hills that make the landscape beautiful.

Biography may be either a help or a hindrance, depending upon how we interpret and apply it. The biographer usually accents the high, stirring moments in the life of his subject and of necessity passes over the days and years when nothing out of the ordinary happened. Yet without the thousands of common days there could have been no continuity between the uncommon ones to bind the life together. In reading the lives of great men we must beware that we do not become dissatisfied with our tame existence and hold lightly the countless treasures which through the mercy of God we all possess. A life that lasted 50 or 70 or 90 years must be condensed into a few pages with the result that the terrain is shoved together and the view distorted. From this out-of-focus picture we are likely to draw three erroneous conclusions: one, that the subject was greater than he actually was; two, that by contrast we are smaller than we really are, and three, that God respects persons and distributes His favors unevenly among His children.

Everything in life is relative, including our blessings. A man who has had the world at his feet may be reduced to a state where he will be grateful for the privilege of sitting 15 minutes in a wheel chair. And the man thus placed who can be as grateful for one gift as for the other has learned the true meaning of Thanksgiving. A man who has been for years totally blind may laugh and weep with thankfulness if at last he recovers but partial sight in one eye. The little polio victim will scream with delight when he discovers that he can run a little bit, even if in doing so he must push an awkward brace along with him. And so with all our lives and all our days. We are always richer than we think.

The conclusion of the matter is simply that we should cultivate the habit of being thankful for small things. Not that we should be less grateful for the great epochal blessings, such as our first radiant sight of the shining kingdom of God in conversion, or deliverance from some physical disease in answer to prayer. These great mountain peaks will always command our attention and stir our hearts to praise. But we must see to it that we do not ignore the humbler blessings.

Personally I am not as strong as Samson, but I'll never cease to thank God I am able to get about over the surface of the earth and attend to the work God has given me to do. I am not a Plato mentally, but I thank God I am sane. I am not rich, but neither am I reduced to beggary. And so with every other blessing the Lord has given me. I hope always to be thankful for the little things; then I'll know what to do with the big ones when God sees fit to send them my way.

CHAPTER

37

God's Blessings Are Found in "The Way"

"I being in the way," explained Eliezer, "the Lord led me." (Genesis 24:27, KJV)

The circumstances were these: When Abraham was old and well stricken in age he called to him his faithful servant Eliezer and commissioned him to go on a long journey into Mesopotamia to procure a wife for Isaac, Abraham's well-beloved son. This was in the far-seeing plan of God and required a man of real faith and consecration to carry it out. The man must have unusual wisdom that he might be led to the right place and fix on the right girl. It looked like a difficult and complicated task, too much indeed for any man to accomplish, but Eliezer came through victoriously. He simply obeyed and God did the rest. He took the appointed way and the Lord led him. It was as simple as that.

Three hundred years later God said to Israel,

"See, I am sending an angel ahead of you to guard you along the way and to bring you to the place I have prepared" (Exodus 23:20). Throughout the Old Testament and on into the New a way is set before men, and over that way the angel of the Lord hovers day and night, guarding and blessing all who faithfully walk in it. They have only to stay in the ordained path to assure the continued fellowship of God.

God's blessing follow the "way" as green vegetation the river. God never varies from the way; He never compromises nor approves a detour. There is just one way, no more, and our present success and future happiness depend upon our finding and following that way.

In the Scriptures the Lord is pictured as a Shepherd walking before His sheep, leading them through the dangerous wilderness of this world. Yet in Isaiah 30:21 it is written, "Your ears will hear a voice behind you, saying, 'This is the way; walk in it.' " Why does the voice of the Lord sound from *behind* us instead of coming as usual from before? The rest of the verse makes it clear, *"whether you turn to the right or to the left."* Whenever we turn our backs on the way, the voice comes from behind us. The Lord never leaves the way. Always His voice sounds in the way and if we wander from it we can only hear a voice behind us, never in front.

The story of the rich young ruler illustrates this further. As Christ watched the young ruler walk away from Him He could speak only from behind him. And as the distance between the two increased, so much more faintly sounded the voice of Jesus in the young man's ears. That was and could be only tragedy for the erring man. Christ calls men to Him. He never leaves the true way to go to them.

Most of the troubles of Christians result from their leaving the way of the Lord to walk in paths of their own choosing. This is justified on the grounds that it is merely an adaptation to the times, a wise adjustment to the changing tastes of modern men. Paul's words, "I am made all things to all men, that I might by all means save some," are lifted out of context and used to give apostolic authority to a bewildering variety of religious frivolities of which prophet or apostle never dreamed. Christians find themselves on unscriptural bypaths far from the plain way of the cross and, assuming they are on the right way, they pray day and night for God to lead them and bless their journey. But their prayers are worse than wasted. By leaving the way of the Lord they cut themselves off from divine assistance. No amount of frantic pleading can save them from disaster.

We can save ourselves a lot of desperate praying for help that never comes if we will but obey the plain teachings of the Scriptures and walk in the way they point out for us. We congratulate ourselves these days that we are more "enlightened" than were those rugged old men of Bible times, but I think we can learn a lot from the man who, more than 3,500 years ago, testified, "I being in the way, the Lord led me."

CHAPTER
38

The Last Sin to Go

The desire for social approbation is one of the less odious self-sins. It has about it nothing of the offensive quality of, say, self-love or self-righteousness. Under certain circumstances it might even be a virtue, for if the world were populated with men and women of pure hearts and holy lives it would be right and natural to want to live in such a manner as to earn their approval.

Undoubtedly those holy beings that inhabit the world above take pleasure in the love and respect of their fellow creatures, but there is and can be no moral parallel between heaven and earth. We dwell in a world halfway between heaven and hell. In hell there is only evil; in heaven there is only good; on earth the tares and wheat grow together, with the tares vastly outnumbering the wheat. There was at least one period in the history of the world when the righteous could be numbered on the fingers of both hands, not counting the thumbs, and the language of Christ gives strong reason to believe that the proportion of good and evil will not be much different at the end of the age (Matthew 24:37–39; Luke 17:26–30).

So corrupt is human nature, so ungodly and rebellious the race of mankind, that the true friend of God is not likely to be accepted by the world, though it sometimes happens that he will be praised for doing something of benefit to society, such, for instance, as the opening up of the interior of Africa by David Livingstone. But the more Christlike men become the surer they are to feel the force of our Lord's words: "If you belonged to the world, it would love you as its own. As it is, you do not belong to the world, but I have chosen you out of the world. That is why the world hates you" (John 15:19); and the words of Paul: "In fact, everyone who wants to live a godly life in Christ Jesus will be persecuted" (2 Timothy 3:12).

To be a true Christian requires that we agree to forfeit the approval of the world. Yet so human are we that this desire to please our fellow men remains with us long after other sins have departed. Mostly we compromise the matter by narrowing the circle of persons whose approval we seek. We write off the sinful worldling as impossible to please and give ourselves no concern about whether or not he approves us. Along with him go the liberal, the modernist, the cultist and a host of others like him. Then we begin to congratulate ourselves that we "fear the face of no man," that we are fearless cross-carrying saints who care nothing for the blame or the praise of men.

Maybe so, but where is the Christian who is actually dead to public opinion? For the most part we are merely dead to the opinion of certain sections of the public, and have preserved to ourselves other smaller groups whose opinion we value very much indeed. I have noticed how this tendency runs throughout all human society. The "highbrow" scorns the favor of the vast majority of mankind, but eagerly courts the favor of his little circle of fellow highbrows and is broken-hearted if they frown upon him. The "society" woman appears to care nothing for the opinion of the millions who read about her shady escapades, but would be driven to suicide if she were excluded from the narrow but select group whose esteem she has come to depend upon as her very life and breath.

Among Christians things are not much different. A preacher earns the reputation of being "fearless" by attacking liberals, Catholics, liquor and immorality, but fawns at the feet of his own little group. He may boldly insult the Pope, but would never dare to cross the monied deacon in his congregation nor express a theological opinion which he knew to be contrary to the mass opinion of the religious group with whom he associates. He is perfectly willing to make enemies of everyone who does not share the opinions of his denomination, but he is careful not to offend anyone in the denomination who is in a position to make him suffer for it.

I cannot believe in the spirituality of any Christian man who keeps an eye open for the approval of others, whoever they may be. The man after God's own heart must be dead to the opinion of his friends as well as his enemies. He must be as willing to cross important persons as obscure ones. He must be ready to rebuke his superior as quickly as those who may be beneath him on the ecclesiastical ladder. To reprove one man in order to gain the favor of another is no evidence of moral courage. It is done in the world all the time.

We'll never be where we should be in our spiritual lives until we are so devoted to Christ that we ask no other approbation than His smile. When we are wholly lost in Him the frantic effort to please men will come to an end. The circle of persons we struggle to please will be narrowed to One. Then we will know true freedom, but not a moment before.

CHAPTER

39

Such Wise Men Are Too Rare

Not much is known about the wise men who came out of the East in search of the newborn King of the Jews, but everything that is known is good. They were "wise men" indeed and checked well on every count.

As far as we know, these men did not have the advantage of a written revelation as did the Jews. They only felt after God in hope that they might find Him, and by His infinite goodness they did find Him. By the dim light of nature, aided perhaps by a tradition borrowed from the Jews, they learned that a Redeemer-King was to come out of Israel and their hearts conceived a great longing to worship Him and to lay some gift at His feet.

Imperfect and sketchy as their faith must have been, God honored it and whispered to them the wondrous news of the approaching Advent. That they were not mere ivory-tower religious dreamers is proved by the fact that they immediately set out to make the long journey, determined to follow the star till it led them to the Savior. Theirs is a good example, and their story a noble and heartening one to meditate upon in this day of universal religious lethargy.

So rich is this story, so replete with lofty and elevating details, that it has been read and told for 20 centuries without exhausting its treasures or dulling the shining luster that surrounds it. Each hearer finds in it something new and fresh each time it is told. But to me at this approaching Christmas season the story of the wise men says two things and says them loudly.

One is that *a longing soul with scanty theological knowledge is in a better position to meet God than a self-satisfied soul, however deeply instructed in the Scriptures.*

The wise men were Gentiles, "being aliens from the commonwealth of Israel, and strangers from the covenants of promise, having no hope, and without God in the world." Yet they saw the star and left all to make the long, dangerous journey to lay worthy gifts at the feet of Jesus. They acted on small knowledge and found the Messiah. That is to their everlasting credit.

On the other hand there were in those days chief priests, high priests, scribes, lawyers, rulers of the synagogues—all keen-eyed students of the Scriptures and experts in the Law and the Prophets; yet as far as we know not one of them had any spiritual awareness that the great day of Israel's visitation had come. They could tell the wise men instantly what the prophets had written about the birthplace of the King, but their knowledge was formal merely. They themselves were blind to its real meaning. Gentiles had to come and rouse them from their strange stupor, if indeed they were ever aroused, for there is little evidence to show that they understood the wise men or knew what all the excitement was about.

The second message the story brings is that *the wise men came to Jesus not to gain something from Him but to give something to Him.*

This circumstance is so unusual as to be almost incredible. We must shake our heads to dispel the clouds from our minds and wait a moment to let our thoughts clear before we can grasp such an idea. It is all so contrary to everything we have been hearing all our lives. Imagine coming to Christ with any other motive than to gain something from Him!

This one act stands almost alone in the life of our Lord. Almost, I say, but not quite, for Mary later broke the alabaster box and poured the precious ointment on His head, and after His crucifixion the two Marys came to look for Him; asking nothing, expecting nothing, but impelled by a selfless love they came to bear His body away. Beyond this there is little evidence of anything as pure and lofty as the worship offered by the wise men. Possibly there was more than we know, and charity would dictate that we at least hope that there was.

One thing that makes the act of unselfish worship appear so beautiful is that it is so rare. Apparently the people of Jesus' day thought of Him as a source of help merely, and it is the "merely" that makes the whole thing questionable. A source of help He was indeed, a fountain in the desert, a star to guide the mariner, bread for the hungry, health for the afflicted and everything that fallen and sinful man can need. Yes, He is our helper, but not our helper *merely*. He is our Lord and our God as well, and infinitely worthy of our ardent, poured-out love and devotion altogether apart from anything He may do for us.

While Christ walked on earth many came to Him, and the motives that brought them were almost as many as they who came. They sought to make Him a king for political gain; they sought preferment for personal ends, as the brothers James and John. They came for healing, for deliverance, for help for themselves, their children and their friends. Among these motives, if some were questionable, others were good and legitimate, but none was wholly free from selfishness of a sort.

Once a leper came to Jesus. In his great distress he could think of only one thing—getting rid of his repulsive sores and becoming a well man again. He came because he wanted something, and the Lord understood and gave it to him. His motive was not the highest, but it was acceptable. Later he came back with a heart full of gratitude and fell on his face to worship Jesus. The first pleased the Lord, no doubt, but the second pleased Him more.

CHAPTER

40

Sure! Pay That Income Tax

A reader of *The Alliance Weekly* (now *Alliance Life*) writes to inquire about the federal income tax. Her question is right to the point, "Should we pay it or not?"

It had never occurred to me that there could be any doubt in anyone's mind about the Christian's obligation toward the income tax, but if one person is troubled about it maybe there are others, so here are a few thoughts, as the political orators say, "along that line."

Spies, feigning themselves just men, once came to Jesus with the question, "Is it lawful for us to give tribute unto Caesar, or no?" These spies were obviously using an honest question to entrap our Lord. The problem they brought to the Savior was one that had been bothering a lot of good people and if it had been asked in sincerity would have been altogether right and proper. Our Lord with His amazing penetration answered the question for all men of good will—and did it without falling into the trap so carefully set for Him.

His answer has become celebrated. "Render therefore unto Caesar the things which are Caesar's, and unto God the things which are God's." Neither the Romans nor the Jewish authorities could object to this injunction, since no one would dare to admit he wanted anything that was not his.

Anyway the word stands, render to governmental authorities whatever by legal right belongs to them. And since they determine what is legally theirs, it is the duty of the Christian to pay—withholding only that over which earthly powers have no right, viz., worship, supreme love and the moral and spiritual claims of the Most High God. These are the things that belong to God alone; and where earthly governments infringe upon them it is and always will be the sacred obligation of every Christian to resist to the death.

Since it is usually not good practice to rest an entire case upon one passage of Scripture, look also at Paul's words to the Roman Christians:

> Everyone must submit himself to the governing authorities, for there is no authority except that which God has established. The authorities that exist have been established by God. Consequently, he who rebels against the authority is rebelling against what God has instituted, and those

> who do so will bring judgment on themselves. . . . Therefore, it is necessary to submit to the authorities, not only because of possible punishment but also because of conscience.
>
> This is also why you pay taxes, for the authorities are God's servants, who give their full time to governing. Give everyone what you owe him: If you owe taxes (tribute in the KJV), pay taxes; if revenue, then revenue; if respect, then respect; if honor, then honor. (Romans 13:1–2, 5–7)

When we remember that "tribute" is *taxes* and is so rendered in many translations, the question of whether or not a Christian should pay his income tax seems no longer to be in doubt. The answer of Christ and Paul is, Yes.

While human governments ("the powers that be") are ordained of God, it does not follow that the rulers or officials of a given country are therefore always just and wise. They can and do err in their judgments and often impose ordinances that are anything but judicious and levy taxes unreasonably high.

It is my opinion that our present federal income tax will prove in the long run to work against the interests of the country. It is altogether possible for a nation to tax itself out of existence. Taxes are absolutely necessary as being the only source of revenue for the maintenance of the government, but when things get so out of hand that it is legally possible for the tax collector (that he has recently become a "director" doesn't make him any the less odious) to take away from a citizen as much as 90 percent of his income, surely history is waving a red lantern in front of us. Unless we slow down we may crash financially and go the way of those nations and empires of yesterday which have left only their crumbling ruins to bear testimony to their departed glory.

What then shall we do? As Christians, pay our taxes exactly as commanded us in the Word of God. As citizens of a democratic country, do whatever we in conscience believe will improve the quality of our leadership and postpone as long as possible the inevitable disaster. And above all things let "requests, prayers, intercession and thanksgiving be made for everyone—for kings and all those in authority, that we may live peaceful and quiet lives in all godliness and holiness" (1 Timothy 2:1–2).

CHAPTER

41

The Law of the Leader

Cattle are driven; sheep are led; and our Lord compares His people to sheep, not to cattle.

It is especially important that Christian ministers know the law of the leader—that he can lead others only as far as he himself has gone. It is of course physically impossible for a shepherd to lead sheep unless he is ahead of them. To attempt to get them into pastures where he has not first gone he could only try to drive them, which would be to confuse them with cattle and to lose his own character as a true shepherd.

The minister must experience what he would teach or he will find himself in the impossible position of trying to drive sheep. For this reason he should seek to cultivate his own heart before he attempts to preach to the hearts of others. If his idea of the green pastures is a lush knowledge of Bible doctrine, he can by hard study and careful teaching lead others as far as he has gone, viz., into a knowledge of doctrine. If he tries to bring them into a heart knowledge of truth which he has not actually experienced he will surely fail. In his frustration he may attempt to drive them; and scarcely anything is so disheartening as the sight of a vexed and confused shepherd using the lash on his bewildered flock in a vain attempt to persuade them to go on beyond the point to which he himself has attained.

There is of course a body of truth that cannot be experienced. By its very nature it can only be received and believed. Such, for instance, is the history recorded in the Bible and all prophetic Scripture yet unfulfilled. There is no way for these truths to be entered into except as we believe them as part of the total redemptive revelations. There is another vast body of truth which can have no final meaning for us except as we experience it. Grace, mercy, forgiveness, cleansing, personal faith in Christ, obedience, cross-carrying, death of the self-life, the infilling with the Holy Spirit, the indwelling of Christ and the walk in the Spirit: these are not doctrines to be believed merely, but spiritual experiences which a given man or woman may or may not enter into personally. These are the truths into which men cannot be driven, but only led by someone who has been there himself.

This law of the leader is demonstrated first in the life of our Lord. He did not and does not drive His people; rather He leads the way Himself and enables His followers to come after Him. He suffered at the hands of men and can therefore fairly ask His people to suffer as He did. While He lived on earth He went about doing good, walking in dignified poverty, and it is no injustice when He calls His followers to lives of frugality and simplicity. He lived in the bosom of the Father even while here below (John 1:18), and led the way for us so we may do the same. He bore His cross and died upon it, so the New Testament requirement of personal crucifixion for all believers is morally logical. Finally, He arose and ascended to sit in heavenly places and thus give foundation to Paul's words in Colossians: "Since, then, you have been raised with Christ, set your hearts on things above, where Christ is seated at the right hand of God. Set your minds on things above, not on earthly things. For you died, and your life is now hidden with Christ in God" (3:1–3).

The law of the leader tells us who are preachers that it is better to cultivate our souls than our voices. It is better to polish our hearts than our pulpit manners, though if the first has been done well and successfully it may be profitable for us to do the second. We cannot take our people beyond where we ourselves have been, and it thus becomes vitally important that we be men of God in the last and highest sense of that term.

What is true for preachers holds true for every Christian witness. Every writer, editor, Sunday school worker, singer, board member and deacon is bound by the law of the leader. He cannot lead where he has not been. Failure in his own life can only mean loss for those who look to him for leadership. Is that why James wrote, "Not many of you should presume to be teachers, my brothers, because you know that we who teach will be judged more strictly" (3:1)? It could be.